Moving Through...

Dawn Elizabeth Waters

Moving Through…Lessons in Grief, Love, Courage, and Making Peace with the Past

Copyright © 2019 by Dawn Elizabeth Waters.

All rights reserved. This book or parts thereof may not be reproduced in any form, stored in any retrieval system, or transmitted in any form by any means—electronic, mechanical, photocopy, recording, or otherwise—without prior written permission of the publisher, except as provided by United States of America copyright law.

For information contact :

High Top Books

http://www.dawnwaters.com

Book and Cover design by Dawn Elizabeth Waters
(Photo Credit: Yvette Waters)

ISBN: 978-1-7334598-1-5

First Edition: September 2019

To Murphy, Shane, and Andrew for always moving through with your momma, despite not having a choice in the matter. To Tony for loving me at my worst, without fail, and being the keeper of my secrets. To Dawn and Ryan for filling my heart with joy and moving through with me, despite having a choice in the matter. Last, but certainly not least, to Yvette and Billy for your legacy in life and death.

Table of Contents

PREFACE 3
1-CANCER SUCKS 9
2-BREATHE. FOCUS. BE PRESENT. 22
3-BECOMING AUTHENTIC 41
4-ASKING THE RIGHT QUESTIONS 49
5-ROADBLOCKS TO AUTHENTICITY 55
6-UNDERSTANDING THE PAST 68
7-NEGATIVITY 86
8-DEALING WITH TRAUMA 91
9-GRIEF 106
10-NEW DAWN. NEW DAY. NEW LIFE. 118
11-FORWARD IS THE DIRECTION HOME 135
12-HELLO ANXIETY 146
13-FEAR IS A LIAR 155
14-COURAGE 167
15-FORGIVENESS 174
16-RELATIONSHIPS 184
17-THE BLAME GAME 193
18-BE YOURSELF 202
19-LOVE YOURSELF 214
20-FINDING PURPOSE 228
21-MINDFULNESS 235
22-PENNIES FROM HEAVEN 243
23-EMBRACE THE JOURNEY 254
24-PARTING WORDS 261

Preface

"Moving through is the constant process of making sense of our journey. We all have a sameness in our struggle, victory, and the challenges we face when doubt, loss, or suffering affects our lives. My story is about overcoming. It is about moving through and embracing the journey. All of it. All the time. It is about hope and coming full circle, even in the most difficult of times. It is about sitting and listening so the lesson sinks in, takes root, and grows into something beautiful, even when it feels horrible and looks ugly. Moving through is a reminder of the healing power of opening up and expressing the deepest parts of yourself. It is also a lesson which teaches that stepping out of the shadows and into the light of the truth is the most sacred gift anyone can give themselves." - Yvette Waters

In the years since *Switching Teams* was published, so much has happened. I told my coming out later in life story and detailed the numerous changes that followed embracing my authentic self. I learned countless lessons about who I am, who I am not, and how life can change at a moment's notice. In my first book, the theme of change was discussed in depth.

In September of 2016, I finally began writing "my next book." The outline was a road map expounding the importance of authentic living and identifying the roadblocks to freedom and peace. My second book would bring to light the reasons why authenticity gets stifled and offer helpful suggestions about how to become more authentic. The goal was to help people forge their own unique path.

At the same time, Yvette founded Braving Life Photography. The intent of the photography project was to honor and capture the beauty of every person fighting to be healthy, strong, and at peace with who they are. Her goal for Braving Life Photography was to create images celebrating the life, courage, and bravery of those dealing with cancer. Her second shoot was for a man who was in home hospice care. She wrote about her experience in a blog dated October 15th, 2016:

"I spent the morning with a wonderful family who are braving life with cancer together. The prognosis for someone diagnosed with stage four colon cancer is not good but the family is making the most of the time they have left with their son, husband, father, father in love, brother, and grandfather.

His daughter "in love", they preferred this descriptor better than in-law, was the one who contacted me and wrote: "Prior to his diagnosis, Bill was never sick a day in his life and has spent the last few years caring for his wife, who has CLL (Chronic Lymphocytic Leukemia). They have spent the better part of a quarter century happily married and taking in life. Bill has 5 grandsons and to say they are his world would be an understatement."

Preface

This was the first time someone reached out to me to photograph someone in home hospice care. When I arrived, Bill's daughter "in love" (again, used instead of in-law) said something that I will remember for a very long time. She shared that her father told her when faced with things you cannot do anything about, find the one small thing that you can do. Calling me was the one small thing she could do.

While there, Bill was a man of few words, but did let everyone know that he was moving one time, and one time only, and said with a grin "I am only doing this once." Even though he was not very talkative, his presence filled the entire house.

While aware of the limited time, they are making every moment count. Because of cancer, the family is choosing not to forget the joy amidst the sadness and grief. They are remaining present and embracing every moment whether sad, joyful, or mundane.

Carving out private family time is a priority, but their home has been open to anyone who wants to spend time with Bill. His wife and mother, both taking turns as caretakers, created and declared the "You will not fall on our watch" rule. They are alternating staying up at night to make sure Bill is not alone and helping him in any way he needs.

In the time I was at the house, there were tears, laughter, humor, serious conversation, grief, and joy. The home was filled with life, despite cancer. When I left, Bill's 14-year-old grandson thanked me for coming. Of course, I pulled out of the driveway teary eyed. Such a sweetheart he was. I was honored to be invited into their world with camera in hand and to learn their story. I left the home thinking about how precious life is and how important it is to live in the moment.

I was reminded today that cancer is not a one man or woman show and affects families as well. I am grateful to this family for their determination and for being such an amazing example of love in action."

In the strangest twist of fate, only two months after launching her cancer project, my wife was diagnosed with breast cancer. It was thirteen days after she wrote the blog. My book took a back seat to tests, surgeries, doctor appointments, and maintaining daily life when cancer moved into our home. In November of 2017, she died unexpectedly of metastatic breast cancer. From the final diagnosis to death was 8 days. Our authentic selves were devastated.

Since then, the original outline has been tweaked, much like life for my family. Strangely enough, the topic of choice did not. Trying to figure out how to incorporate everything and stay true to the message was a challenge. Finding the motivation to be thoughtful and write again took a long time.

The title of the book changed. "Not Broken" turned in to "Moving Through" and is a tribute not only to Yvette, but to every person who keeps going forward fearlessly despite adversity, trauma, or tragedy. Learning how despair and joy can exist in the same space simultaneously is a lesson we all can benefit from.

The story of Yvette's life was not mine to tell until now. Oddly, her story is universal. Her legacy is a lesson and reminder of how life can hurt but can also be healed by doing the hard things. Moving through is more than an idea for a tattoo, the title of a personal art project, thirteen letters on a page, or two words spoken aloud. It is a necessary part of a life well lived.

Preface

Two words. Thirteen letters. Moving through. What do these words mean to you? Prior to October of 2016, these words were just letters on a page. In February of 2017, they came to represent courage and hope, courtesy of a brave woman who was recovering from a cancer diagnosis and double mastectomy. This woman happened to be a photographic genius and a talented artist who accepted the challenge from a mentor and friend to go deeper with her art and tell her story. Thanks, Blue Star. Without the sarcasm this time. Honestly.

The process of creating her project was challenging. The struggle mirrored her life. I always thought my late wife's story was better suited for a book because it was filled with an abundance of teachable moments. She would have none of it. Convincing her to tell her story took 47 years. Her life was the total package, even though it ended much sooner than expected. There are things that may be hard to read and details which have not been publicly shared. There is a fine line between guarding privacy and sharing the lessons born out of her life and death.

She was tough and tender. The combination served her well. Her fiery spirit brought her through many dark times, and she was unbreakable. Regardless of the struggle, love emanated from her being. Even at her own expense at times.

The love she had for others was remarkable yet finding that love for herself was often a challenge. These positions fought with each other for the entirety of her life. Ever an optimist, her mission was seeking peace for the world with the hopes it would permeate her wounded spirit and bring healing.

Her quest for peace was evident in her photographs. She managed to capture complex emotions in the simplest of photographs, all the while working through her own maze of trauma through the lens of her camera.

Her talent spoke for itself. Her personality was contagious and genuine. I wanted to be her when I grew up. We all have heroes and role models. She was mine. She still is. This woman also happened to be my wife, and best friend of seventeen years. "What would Yvette do" is a question asked daily by our family. Her loss is felt every day, but because of her courage and bravery we continue to move through our journey knowing she is here in spirit.

It took four months to be able to sit down and write coherently. Truth be told, to write anything at all. The last thing I typed was the obituary for my wife's celebration of life in December 2017.

With hindsight and time, moments of clarity returned and allowed my brain to finally unclench and my fingers to return to the keyboard. Like fingers moving across a keyboard, life marches on. Moving forward, and through, takes patience, fortitude, and a willingness to embrace life despite pain, loss, or the story of the past that leaves its mark.

Usually a story has a beginning, middle, and an end. In order to understand the beginning sometimes you must work backwards from the end. Yvette always read the last page of a book before she went to the beginning. The end is where this story begins.

1 - CANCER SUCKS

First things first. Some background is necessary to fully comprehend the events leading up to the end. Yvette Marie Waters' family history of cancer was well documented by her physicians. Her maternal grandmother had breast cancer, five years of remission, then it returned and metastasized to her bones. In 1991, she passed at the age of 65. Yvette was 22. Her grandmother was her safe place and coping with the loss was not easy. Her maternal grandfather was diagnosed with lymphoma and died at the age of 70. Her mother was diagnosed with colon cancer in 2009 and had surgery; however five years later it came back and had metastasized to her stomach, brain and colon. She was 65 when she died.

Her family history made her vigilant about getting mammograms and ultrasounds of her dense breasts from the age of 30. In March of 2016, her annual exam was painful. No ultrasound was ordered. There was a large lump which was visible to naked eye at 12 o'clock position which was determined to be a cyst/calcification. She was advised to come back next year.

In September 2016, a smaller cyst was noticed at 1 o'clock position and was next to the large mass. She went to her primary care doctor to ask for another mammogram. The results of those indicated an ultrasound was needed. It took two weeks to schedule the ultrasound. The small cyst was of no concern, but the large cyst required a biopsy. The same cyst which was fine six months earlier was suddenly sending up red flags.

On October 28th, 2016, she was diagnosed with Invasive Ductal Carcinoma, Grade 2, ER/PR positive HER2 negative breast cancer. Next steps included a consultation with a nurse and setting up appointments with the surgeon, oncologist, and radiology oncologist to become established as a patient pending further typing of tumor and course of action.

Her surgeon reviewed the previous mammograms and was shocked that no biopsies were done earlier given the size of the mass. On November 23rd, an MRI was performed in preparation for a double mastectomy. The surgery took place on December 6th. The hospital report and pathology indicated a 4.5 x 4 x 2.5cm mass of poorly differentiated invasive ductal carcinoma. During the surgery, two sentinel nodes were removed, and the surgeon indicated clear margins. Drainage tubes were removed the following week.

While she recovered, we waited for the pathology report and the tumor type test to come in. At the end of the month we met with the surgeon, who told us her ONCA-Dx type score was 24. The threshold for needing chemo was a 25. The chance of recurrence was 85/15 with tamoxifen. On January 5th, 2017, she had an appointment with the oncologist to get the tamoxifen prescription. She saw a nurse practitioner. As she was leaving, the nurse practitioner said her doctor wanted to speak with her. He advised a precautionary course of chemo but also said she fell in a gray area. The numbers and data only indicated an additional 2-3% improvement of the 85/15. After further consultation with her surgeon, Yvette decided against chemo.

Her surgeon fully supported the decision. A month later, she went for her annual OB/GYN appointment and this doctor was shocked to learn of the breast cancer diagnosis and surgery. To be safe, she ordered an ultrasound of her ovaries to make sure nothing was going on. Two cysts on each ovary were noted and she was advised to have a repeat ultrasound in three months.

Cancer was not invited, but it took up residence in our house. Surgery may have removed the tumor, along with both of her breasts, but it did not evict the unwelcomed tenant. Every day we felt it, some days more than others. Work, kids, and daily routines offered momentary distractions from thinking about cancer, but it never disappeared for long.

When this new roommate snuck in unannounced and became a squatter under our roof, our lives were altered. When cancer moved in, it brought luggage that cluttered every square foot of the house and consumed our favorite snacks unapologetically. It hijacked the security system, disabled the motion detectors, and blacked out the camera views. It was not seen, but its presence was undeniable.

At night, it roamed the floors interrupting the quiet and, in the morning, made daylight feel suffocating. Its mission was to steal the valuables, rummage through the closets, and leave things in disarray. It stuck to the fibers of our clothes, dripped from the walls, and followed us out the door and into the world.

The universe denied my repeated requests for an easy button to appear in the days before and the day of her surgery. I felt helpless and sick to my stomach thinking about what was happening down the hall from where I sat waiting. Fear, anger, and sadness galloped around my brain continuously.

Thoughts of disbelief and worry about how her recovery would be impacted by her allergies to pain medication cramped my brain. Her worries were for me and how I would do while waiting for her. Even in the face of her disease, her thoughts were for my well-being.

Prior to her surgery, my wife frequently referred to it as the day her boobs were getting chopped off. This was a disturbing but true representation of facts. As the mastectomy got closer, I reached down deep and became the voice of optimism. I suggested an alternative description and began referring to it as the day she would not have cancer growing inside her body.

Staying positive was the least I could do, even though we both secretly worried about what else was inside of her waiting to start growing. When someone gets diagnosed with cancer, so do their family, friends, and loved ones. She often reminded me that we both had cancer, but our experiences were dissimilar.

Daily life changed once cancer knocked on the door. Fighting was more courageous than waving the white flag, right? Head down and one foot in front of the other is a great approach, however it is not fool proof.

Few areas of life were unaffected. Grocery shopping was not as fun as it used to be. Reading labels and making choices to reduce the chance of anything we ate causing future cancers to pop up was routine. Our vigilance was heightened to the point of obsession.

Sitting and watching television was no longer enjoyable or an escape. Until cancer came calling, we were unaware of the frequency and volume of cancer-related commercials and story lines in our shows. Our sympathy became empathy.

While grateful only medication was needed, we wrestled with conflicting emotions. Gratitude. Anger. Gratitude. Disbelief. Gratitude. Fear. Gratitude. Sadness. All at once. We wondered if anger squashed gratitude. Can they exist simultaneously?

We stuffed emotions and privately talked ourselves out of our own grieving process. Partly because we worried about how our feelings would affect the other but mostly because it felt too overwhelming.

Slowly, we maneuvered through the maze of emotions and allowed ourselves to vent, cry, and laugh. It was a work in progress with no definite ending point. Cancer changed our priorities and dominated the conversation. We were doing okay, yet there were times when we were not as okay as we thought we were. Removing the cancer was the easy part. Working through the lingering emotions and wading through the mental impact lasted long past the physical recovery and treatment.

The changes to my wife's body were classified as cosmetic. Although her identity was not tied up in her breasts, losing them changed more than just how she appeared in a sweater. Women who lose their breasts to cancer must sort through more than their closets to find new clothing which fits their new shape. They worry about whether their spouse will still be attracted to them and whether they are considered real women anymore. Adjusting to life without a part of your body takes time. Getting past the anger and sadness takes longer. Grieving the loss of breasts is not something that is often discussed openly. In fact, it has been difficult to research or verbalize to anyone. Why?

One theory is the fear of being shallow, selfish, or getting lumped in with those who bail on marriages or relationships after their partner has a mastectomy. It happens more than you think. Who wants to be a jerk? Not me. How could I complain or feel badly when my wife was doing well? Not me. What were the rules for feeling upset my wife lost her breasts? There were none. A quick Google search on the topic of lesbian double mastectomy grieving shows nothing. Zero. Surprisingly, little insight exists for men whose wives lose their breasts to cancer either, save a few sentences about the importance of supporting your spouse when a health crisis arises.

I came up with my own rules. As I tried to sort through the feelings, I realized I was asking the wrong questions and changed direction. Did I fall in love with her because of her breasts? No. Did losing her breasts change who she was? No. Was she less of a woman because she no longer had breasts? Hell no. Did she know I thought she was more beautiful than ever? No.

The truth was my wife was not, and never had been, just her breasts. This conclusion was not a tough one to reach. Having said that, there were a few more questions which needed answering. Did I miss my wife's breasts? Yes. Did I wish we, meaning myself and her boobs, had more than six years together before she was diagnosed? Absolutely. In fact, I felt like this was a cruel joke, especially given our late in life coming out story.

It took six months for me to understand these were perfectly acceptable feelings and feeling that way did not make me an asshole. More than the loss of her breasts, we grieved the loss of what life was like before cancer and the reality of life after cancer.

Which brings us to the million-dollar question. Do I wish cancer got lost on the way to our address? More than anything. This was the main source of my anger and sadness. Everything else stemmed from there. Her breasts were just a casualty of a shitty disease.

Yvette had my full support when she chose not to have reconstruction. In fact, I asked her to consider not having it. Either way, cancer happened, and a new set of boobs was not going to help us forget about it. Reconstruction meant more surgeries, and recoveries, and drainage tubes, and bras. My wife became a proud member of the flat and fabulous club.

In addition to her physical appearance, her mental and emotional state changed. Surprisingly, despite the shock of looking in a mirror and the reminder of what happened, she felt more at peace than ever.

Understanding life brings moments of joy and tribulation and accepting how these opposing feelings exist simultaneously throughout is hard. On better days, we saw how dealing with cancer renewed our commitment to live life fearlessly. On decent days it reminded us of what was important and to let go of the things which could hinder our growth.

The moments of feeling self-conscious were eventually met with determination and gratitude. Neither of us were ready to put getting cancer in the blessing category. Cancer may have taken from us, but it also gave us a greater appreciation for one another and life in general.

As a lesbian couple, the discomfort many already have with our "lifestyle" choice has not gone unnoticed by either of us. Unfortunately for some of our family and "friends", adding cancer to the mix did little to adjust their perception or foster understanding about the similarities between same sex and heterosexual relationships.

Cancer did not care what lifestyle was "chosen" or who we decided our person to love was. However, it was an opportunity to learn how to take the good with the bad. The paint on our house may have faded and our windows may have lacked shine, but we persevered. We had a squatter lurking in our midst but never saw what happened next coming. The other side of cancer never happened for us, yet our commitment to move forward every day was unshaken.

She began complaining about hip pain but attributed it to a skeletal issue from childhood. One of her legs was slightly longer than the other. At the end of March 2017, an ultrasound of her ovaries showed 2 cysts. A six week follow up ultrasound was ordered to check the size and check for notable changes.

The next weekend she photographed a wedding and was still feeling fatigued as her recovery from surgery continued. It was her first large event post-surgery. The following Monday she had a follow up appointment with the oncologist. The team of doctors met regularly to update each other and report on patient progress.

He entered the room without a chart and asked if there were any questions and said "well, some people think you are going to be fine." Deciding against chemo changed his demeanor. He was upset the prophylactic course of treatment was not embraced by her. We fired him and transferred her files to a different oncologist.

At her three month follow up with the surgeon, a mass on her thyroid was discovered. Another ultrasound ordered. She asked about the possibility of having a PET scan to make sure everything was okay. Request denied. She was terrified of the cancer spreading without warning and was afraid of it killing her. Later that day, she met with the new oncologist. He reviewed her file, discussed the thyroid discovery and ran labs. Also discussed was her decision to forego "just to be safe" chemo based on the risk versus benefits of falling in the middle of the statistics. He agreed the Tamoxifen course was enough.

Once again, she asked the oncologist about ordering a PET scan. He assured her that labs coming back within normal limits did not warrant further evaluation and told her being afraid is normal.

In July of 2017, the thyroid biopsy was performed, and the results showed the sample to be benign. However, even that result was only 80/20. Soon after, she began a new full-time job working at Se7en Bites Bake Shop in Orlando. Every day she came home exhausted and slept. She attributed it to her thyroid issue and working full time outside of the house for the first time in a long time. She cut back on her photography business and photographing extended conventions because she was too fatigued to do it. At the end of August, she commented often about feeling bloated and uncomfortable in her abdominal area. Upon further research, these were common side effects of tamoxifen and quitting smoking. My concern was growing by the day, but Yvette powered through and kept going. She was stubborn that way.

At the beginning of September, there was another follow up with the oncologist and more labs were drawn. All were within normal range. The fatigue continued and her energy was non-existent. Two days after Hurricane Irma hit our area, she came down with an upper respiratory infection and bronchitis which required a trip to the primary care physician. It was September 15th. She explained her fatigue and fear of every ache and pain being cancer coming back. Again, she was reassured that it was natural to feel that way after being diagnosed. She was given an antibiotic.

Two weeks later she quit Se7en Bites. It was too much. She was exhausted and felt like she was in a fog. Her concern grew as the aches and pains in her back and abdomen became more pronounced. Her ribs hurt, which she attributed to the lingering nerve pain from surgery. She was a light smoker after her surgery but quit for good in July when the thyroid issue was discovered.

By the end of September, Yvette found it difficult to sleep when lying flat. Some nights she slept in a chair in the living room. On October 24th, 2017, she was feeling awful and experiencing shooting pains in her ribs, back, hip, and abdominal area. Once again, she made an appointment with the primary care physician. Yvette again explained her fatigue, fear, and paranoia about cancer returning. She also reminded the physician's assistant that she quit smoking. The doctor ordered a chest x-ray to make sure nothing was going on because of her history of smoking. The chest x-ray came back normal.

Two days later she had a follow up with the surgeon. Her fatigue was once again the topic of conversation. The surgeon suggested she take ESTER-C to boost her immune system to help the healing process. According to Yvette the thyroid results were also reviewed. I was not at that appointment, so had no idea what was discussed other than buying the ESTER-C.

She continued to suffer from fatigue and random pains. She was convinced the issues were her body getting used to not smoking.

Her abdomen was getting large and she was putting on excess weight. Another side effect of tamoxifen. Yvette also began complaining of nausea after eating and spent the better part of October and November trying to find foods that did not make her feel ill afterward. I noticed her zoning out and trying to manage her pain, yet she still pushed herself. She did not understand why nothing was making her feel better and why quitting smoking would be making her feel so awful.

I remember she looked washed out and noticed her skin color was slightly off. She was tired and silently struggling with the pain every day. My wife was a tough woman who had a very high pain tolerance, but I knew she was in constant pain and just wanted to feel better.

She had a wedding gig scheduled on November 11th, 2017 and did it alone. When she came home, she said her hip gave out after bending down. She was not sure why this happened but managed to get up and continue with the event. I was concerned and kept asking if we should go to the ER. She reminded me she had been to docs and they did not seem to think anything was bad enough to require any scans or tests.

After the wedding, she was barely eating anything. She felt terrible. She thought if she could just rest, she could feel better. I noticed the whites of her eyes had a yellow tinge to them on November 15th but did not say anything. I knew the following day she had an appointment with the primary care physician. On November 16th, before leaving for the appointment, she mentioned her urine had been a weird color intermittently for a couple of weeks. News to me. She suspected the abdominal and back pain, nausea, and the dark urine meant she might have a urinary tract infection.

She told the doctor about her rib pain. He had no answer for what it could be. She also pointed out her bloated abdomen and gave a urine sample. He diagnosed her with a urinary tract infection due to the presence of bilirubin, white blood cells, and blood. He did mention that she might want to get her gall bladder checked. He said no rush; it could wait until after the Thanksgiving holiday. She called when she got home and made an appointment for Tuesday, November 22nd. After she returned home, I asked if he mentioned the color of her skin or eyes. She said he did not but wanted her to get an ultrasound of her gall bladder.

On Saturday, November 17th, she struggled to get out of bed for our son's soccer game. I told her to rest. Later that afternoon she looked at me and asked me to take her to the ER at Fish Memorial Hospital in Orange City, Florida. She could barely walk and was in excruciating pain. We thought it was a gall bladder attack. After intake and tests, she was officially diagnosed with metastatic breast cancer and sepsis of unknown origin. There were "innumerable masses on her liver, spine, pelvis, femur, skull, and fluid at the base of her lungs." Her abdomen was distended from metastatic fluid. She was admitted immediately.

2 - BREATHE. FOCUS. BE PRESENT.

One week. That was it. In the moment, it is hard to remember cancer is the reason why your best friend and love of your life is throwing and landing punches on your face. It is even harder to not completely fall apart while trying to comfort and calm down the person you love most in the world as the dying process escalates. In life she was passionate and was known to be quite feisty when upset. There was no way in hell to expect my wife would go gently into that good night.

Although we had two days to say everything we thought we needed to say, there was so much left unsaid. The night in the cold ER when the diagnosis was made was like a business meeting. We thought we would have time to get our brains aligned with the reality of the situation. The truth is we never said goodbye to one another. It was that quick. Between the medication, sepsis, jaundice, and pain, the lucid moments were few and far between.

Breathe. Focus. Be Present.

We reviewed the game plan, verbally vomited on one another, said everything running through our minds. It was the best we could do to encourage one another in the face of the worst possible news someone can hear. You are dying. She assured me I could do this, and I assured her she was the strongest person I had ever known. She apologized for being sick. I ignored the apologies and reminded her of every trip we took and special moments we shared in the seven years we were together. Even in her diminished mental state, she was upset with herself for putting our family through this.

Being the cause of suffering for someone was her greatest nightmare and challenging for her to process. Her internal dialogue was clouded by a life that was not always easy. Her baggage was not garden variety, but she kept pushing through every day the best she could.

She was not ready to hear that the cancer had metastasized and less ready to begin to wrap her brain around the speed in which the end would come. She had enough time to send messages to a few friends the first night she was admitted. Each message pleaded for assurance that I would not be alone in this journey.

She gave detailed, shit, very detailed, instructions about her wishes and I promised to follow through on every one of them. Although cancer was ravaging her body, it did not steal her sense of humor. When the doctor left the room, she told me she had a confession to make. "I am a pen thief!" This was not news to me based on the pile of random pens littering our home. I told her I knew, and it was okay. There were worse things.

Within 24 hours of being admitted she would be rendered incapable of doing anything other than lying in a bed and was already in the process of dying. The hope was never for recovery, but rather effective pain management.

Breathe. Focus. Be Present. These were the rules. Rules which prevented me from being reduced to a puddle on the floor next to my wife's bedside. The six-day mantra kept me grounded and focused on helping her endure what would be her final week on earth.

The day after she was admitted my angel appeared at the door of the hospital room. It was Sunday. Tony did not have wings or a halo, but he was every bit of my saving grace and grounding person. The loss of his own spouse unexpectedly only four months prior did not stop him from being my rock as he grappled with his own grief.

I felt conflicted asking him to come and be there with me. When he arrived, I stepped out of the room and greeted him with apologies. He laughed and told me not to be ridiculous. He and I met at a Pride event and were introduced by his husband, Billy, who was a force in in own right and well known, and loved, in Orlando. We clicked instantly. He is my brother from another mother.

The next words I spoke to him were with tears running down my cheeks. I told him I didn't think I could do this. His response was simple. Breathe. Focus. Be present. He put his hands on my shoulder and took a deep breath with me. Next, Tony put my face in his hands and repeated those four words. It caught me off guard.

Breathe. Focus. Be Present.

I was fully expecting a pep talk and not wisdom that would change my entire approach to the hell we were experiencing.

Our kids came to visit that afternoon. She spent the morning vomiting after trying to eat the breakfast they brought. She was hell bent on getting better. Not even her determination could stop the inevitable. Fortunately, the nausea stopped before the boys arrived. She was ushered in and out of the room for multiple MRI's and CT scans. While she was gone, we just looked at each other and made small talk. It was surreal. Our youngest son remembers her offering him a blanket because the room was cold. Our oldest gently spoke to her and held her hand before he left.

The parade of doctors began before she was brought back to the room. The oncologist asked if we were all family and if it was okay to discuss the findings with everyone there. Our hearts dropped as he spoke. The avalanche of bad news sucked the air from the room. The cancer was engulfing her liver and had spread to her stomach, spine, pelvis, and skull. The official diagnosis was metastatic breast cancer.

This visit would be the last time the boys spoke to her. Timing. Our oldest came down with strep a day later and was not able to work or visit. He had moved out only four months before. Our middle son came to the hospital every day to check on us both. Our youngest held down the fort and stayed with the dog all week. She was his second mom, and this was a lot for a 14-year-old to absorb. I let him decide if he wanted to visit. Every night I updated him and with every passing day the news became less optimistic. Watching him process what was happening broke my already breaking heart more.

The plan Sunday was to begin aggressive chemotherapy hoping it would offer some relief and give her a chance. The doctor also said it could kill her. I asked if we were putting a drop of water on a forest fire. Chemo seemed silly because of how far everything had progressed. A biopsy of her liver was scheduled for Tuesday. She mentioned waiting to get biopsy results before agreeing to chemo. A port was scheduled to be placed Monday, but never happened.

Why, you ask? The port insertion was cancelled by my wife while I had stepped out to make a phone call. I found out when the charge nurse told me the patient, who was on morphine and other pain meds, cancelled it. I was furious.

The biopsy paperwork consent was the last time she signed her name. While the biopsy was being performed, I ran home to get the power of attorney and health care surrogate papers we created after we married. My return trip to the hospital was delayed because I got pulled over by police near my house. Great. I burst in to tears and explained my rush. I got a stern talking to and was let go with a warning.

On Tuesday evening I asked the nurse to hold off on the morphine so I could try to speak with her and ask what she wanted to do. She was confused, scared, and did not understand why she was not getting better. When she was first diagnosed, we discussed what to do in such a circumstance. She did not want treatment for a terminal illness. Her wishes were clearly indicated in the health care surrogate paperwork. This predetermined course of action did not stop her from asking me why I wanted to kill her when the option of doing nothing was brought up.

Handing the healthcare surrogate paperwork to the nurse was hard. From that morning on nothing could be done without my permission and knowledge. I summoned the on-call oncologist and again asked if chemo was going to do anything or give her any chance of recovery. I struggled knowing what to do. While not a doctor, I knew what was happening. She was incoherent and becoming agitated with the blood draws and needle sticks to administer her nausea meds.

Further complicating life was the stupid wrist band on her arm which prevented the phlebotomist from drawing blood from her arms. We learned in the ER that anyone who had a double mastectomy was not supposed to have blood pressure taken or blood drawn from their arms. News to us. Frankly, she had bigger problems to deal with and her condition was critical. For three days I argued with nurses and finally got one who was willing to give the nausea meds via her IV. It was not protocol but in this case an exception was made. Having the meds go directly in the veins and the possible irritation which could result was the least of her worries at that point. Yes, I was a nightmare spouse and got loud and insistent on more than one occasion.

Our last embrace came after an arduous attempt to use the bedside commode on Tuesday. As I tried to lift her, she let go of the side rails and reached up toward my midsection. My eyes welled up with tears and in that moment, I knew she was reaching out to me for the last time. I could see determination and worry in her beautiful green eyes. Finding a way to work around the limitations of her body was her final act of love. The pseudo hug lasted a few moments before her arms dropped to her side.

Breathe, focus, be present saved me from missing this moment of light in the darkness. After the port debacle, the plan became to administer chemo via IV. It was not ideal. News flash, none of this was. It was Wednesday night. The order was finalized, and chemo was set to begin on Friday morning, the day after Thanksgiving. Between the morphine, anti-nausea medication, and the cancer, communication was problematic. She stopped checking her phone the day after being admitted and was unable to stand up on her own by Tuesday.

Midweek, I held her hand while she dreamed of long past relatives and selfishly hoped a few more lucid moments would happen. Her trust in me superseded her own stubborn will. The moments she relied on me to literally hold her up were fueled by my hope to give her some relief from the pain coursing through her cancer ravaged body.

Breathe. Focus. Be Present. This intentional mantra played on a loop in my head and was the only way to circumvent the pain in my heart watching her suffer. While hard, the time spent next to her was sacred. Whispering words of love in her ear when I felt myself becoming overwhelmed with the gravity and reality of watching her life slipping away brought some moments of peace. I played music when my tears prevented me from talking.

Breathe. Focus. Be Present.

Powerless to change the outcome, I had to dig deep to find a purpose amid the quiet chaos found on the fifth floor of the hospital. The last two days were the most trying. As her body fought pain, she fought me. Her fighting spirit did not go unnoticed. The woman I knew and loved was fighting her body and its betrayal of her longevity.

When she asked flat out if she was dying, my reply was not a yes or no. Instead, I told her we were all dying. As the meds kicked in, my ritual was to step out of the room to breathe, focus, and be present. Morphine was her saving grace. Phenergan was the icing on her comfort cake. As she rested, I held her hand and continued to talk to her as she floated between this world and the next. There just was not enough time. It was that quick. There were panicked moments when I realized I forgot something I wanted to tell her. The clock was not our friend. Cancer is a quick little bastard.

I began every attempt to talk to her with "I Love You." Sometimes she said it, but speech was an arduous task. Even though her mouth could not make the words, her yellowed eyes said it when they periodically opened. I would have given anything to know what she was thinking, if she knew I was next to her, and that I loved her more than anything. I wiped her mouth when swallowing her saliva became impossible. Even though her body was failing, she managed a grin when I joked about "getting her pants off" to use the bedside commode.

The last time she said, "I Love You" happened on Thanksgiving Day and was a softly whispered mumble of "Wi Wuf Yew." I told her she sounded like Elmer Fudd. Again, another smirk. Our last kiss happened shortly after. It took everything she had to conjure up that valiant effort to pucker up.

While she rested my mind wandered. The unfinished plans, future projects, and recently bought concert tickets occupied my thoughts. I listened to her breathe and memorized her face when I was not staring out the window watching the world go by. There were so many questions but no answers that registered or made sense. Why? Is this all there is to life? Seven years was not enough time together. Existential questions would have to wait. Breathe. Focus. Be present.

Thursday was the worst day. It was also Thanksgiving. Great. Cancer does not care what time of the year it is, or which holiday is being disrupted. The skeleton crew and giant plate of turkey with fixings the cafeteria delivered to her room was a kick in the gut. Her feet and arms were like ice cubes. I could not understand why the medical team did not see what I was seeing. Our dear friend Heriot came by and sat with us. He sweetly held her hand and hung his head as he prayed for her.

Her mom died of colon cancer only four years prior. Our hospice education taught that cold limbs were indicators of the dying process. Why was no one listening? Science was running the show and nothing short of Jesus appearing and healing her body was going to change the outcome. I reached my breaking point about the wrist band situation and summoned the charge nurse to cut them from her arms. This is the politest way to describe the interaction since admittedly I was in full on asshole mode

Breathe. Focus. Be Present.

advocating for my wife. By summoned, I mean demanded angrily that it happen.

On Friday morning I had an obligation to attend to and asked her best friend Jen to come from out of town to sit with her until I could get there. The circus that happened while I was gone still haunts me. In the two hours I was away, bloodwork showed her potassium was too high to begin the chemo. Great. Administering the treatment with high potassium levels could cause a heart attack. Perfect.

To remedy the issue, she was given something to help pull potassium out of her blood and eliminate it via her stool. Sounds reasonable right? No. She had not gone to the bathroom in two weeks and this was just dumb. She was force fed the drink. She tried to get out of bed and leave a few times that morning. When I arrived, she was pissed and completely out of it.

I sat in the chair and felt sick. What were we doing? She did not want this. None of it. The final confirmation of what I was already wrestling with all week came when her nurse for the morning came on shift. He walked in the door and stopped. The door on the room was draped with signs for impending chemo. I looked up at him and his face was blank.

He took one step toward me and just shook his head and said quietly "What are we doing?" I felt like someone else finally saw what I was seeing all week. She was dying. Doctors are in the business of saving lives and doing whatever they can to help people heal. I get it. All the conversations she and I had about what to do if or when something like this were to happen rolled through my head all week. This ship was sinking, and she was suffering.

The hospital was not treating her but making her comfortable during her time there. My friend Jaime came to see us later that morning. Jaime also was a board member for a non-profit organization, The Barber Fund, which helps those living, and dying, from cancer. Jaime also sat with me while Yvette was having her surgery. Timing. We spoke at length about what was happening as I walked her to the parking lot. After she left, I walked toward the elevator on my way back to the fifth floor. I knew it was time to make some decisions.

I stood outside of the room for a moment and took a deep breath. Her sister and best friend were still inside. I asked them to step outside. I needed to speak with them. We stood in the hallway and I told them it was time. They agreed that she did not want this, and the decision was made to sign a DNR and call hospice. Signing the DNR crushed my soul.

I called the oncologist and let them know the decision. They did not argue but made sure I understood what this meant. I did. Before I hung up the phone, the nurse came in and discovered the IV line had collapsed her vein. We waited all afternoon for the special IV team to come in and start a new one. When they arrived, a central line in her upper left arm was the only option available.

The process was gut wrenching. I agreed to the central line only because she would be spared any more needles poking her when she arrived at hospice. Yvette was suffering enough. It was the least

Breathe. Focus. Be Present.

I could do. Two phlebotomists with a camera came in and began to work. She was not happy at all. She was incoherent yet in pain. I was on the bed keeping her chest pinned down and holding her right arm to keep her from swinging. Being restrained was on her list of hell no, never, activities. The entire time I whispered in her ear to lay still. Her best friend held her legs while marveling at the wonders of science and the vein radar tool. I was not thinking about anything other than making it through this shitty procedure.

The insertion of the line took 30 minutes. I told her it would stop hurting if she stayed still and continually whispered how much I loved her. I was sweating and holding back tears the entire time. Once the IV line was placed, hospice arrived with the paperwork. What the hell was happening? I remember thinking how fucked up this was. The weight of everything felt crushing. Waking up from this nightmare was not going to happen.

She was "going home" the next day. Which was dry erase board hospital speak for being moved to hospice. I called the kids and told them they needed to come home. The dread and disbelief were paralyzing. I returned home from the hospital and told them the worst news any parent could. She was dying. Our oldest, who is very stoic, burst into tears. The three of us looked at him and each other. His breaking down made it real. We cried for a long time and promised to be there for each other.

I arrived at the hospital early the next morning to wait for transport. They told me it would happen at 2pm. Ugh. I crawled in bed with her and stared at her face until her vitals were taken at noon. I sat in the chair beside her when she became agitated. A short time later, a young nurse came in and greeted me. She unfolded a sterile kit and set in on the foot of the bed. I asked her what she was going to do.

"Take out the IV" she said. I stood up. Motioned for her to turn around and instructed her to go talk to the nurse. She told me "patients usually do not go to hospice with a central line." I told her I didn't care what usually happens. There was nothing "usual" about any of this. Again, full on asshole mode. She left and never came back. After the trauma of placing the line, there was no way in hell it was coming out. Or as she would say, no fucking way. I even channeled her mother when I instructed her to go "fetch" the charge nurse.

The transport arrived and took her to the hospice facility near the hospital. By 3 p.m. she was settled in and people began arriving to see her. More paperwork. As the afternoon sun dipped behind the trees, she was surrounded by so many who she touched. She laid in the bed looking peaceful and unaware of what was happening in the room. But I knew she could hear us laughing and hoped she was feeling the love. Later that night, our friend Mama B came by and just wanted to sit with us. The room was quiet when the doctor made his rounds. Her breathing was becoming shallower, but he said she was comfortable and not in any pain.

I was bracing for the worst to start. When her mom was in hospice, shallow breathing was followed by the death rattle. I did not hear that yet, so I thought going home to get some rest would be safe to do. When I left for home, I kissed her on the forehead and told her I would see her tomorrow. Mama B stayed. I left around 11:30 p.m.

Breathe. Focus. Be Present.

and went home to a house I knew she would never step foot in again. I sat on the couch and stared at the television while our oldest snoozed on the couch beside me.

At 2:35 a.m. I realized my phone was ringing. The phone was propped up beside my head on a pillow. I must have dozed off. I did not recognize the number on the phone. Then it registered. Foggy, I answered thinking it was going to be the "come now, it is time" call. It was her hospice nurse but not the call I expected. She was gone. She told me Mama B left around 1:30 a.m. Thirty minutes later she went in to shift her position and noticed she looked so at peace, and beautiful. It took her a moment to realize she was not breathing. She began calling me then. It was 2 a.m.

The air left my lungs and my heart sunk. I asked her what I needed to do next. She told me I could come, and they would do whatever I wanted. I knew nothing in that moment except that I was in shock and not sure I wanted to see her gone.

I hung up the phone and was frozen. I glanced down and saw five missed calls from hospice prior to the one I heard. To this day, I do not know how I did not hear the phone ringing next to my ear. I got up off the couch, went into my bathroom, and called Blue. She was a mentor of Yvette's, the founder of The Barber Fund, and a dear friend.

I remember stringing together many fucks and just babbling. I asked her if it was shitty of me to not want to see her gone. She told me I could do whatever I wanted and asked if the boys had been told. I hadn't done anything except get up off the couch and sit on the bathroom floor. Blue told me I had to tell them and lovingly told me to get up off the floor and do this. I hung up and shared the news.

I debated going back to hospice for what seemed like hours. But as I was deciding, I realized my shoes were on and the car keys were in my hand. The first night in the ER I had asked her if she wanted me to be there when it happened. Her response was "I would like you to be, but if you are not, it is okay." I did not realize how much relief that answer would bring once it happened.

I drove to hospice crying the entire way. Memories of rushing to hospice when her mother died invaded my thoughts. We had nicknamed this building the death place in 2014. When I arrived, I found her nurse, who relayed the same information from earlier. I thanked her and she told me to take as much time as I needed. I stood at the closed door and prepared myself. The sadness forced the air from my lungs. I still remember the cold draft that met my face when I opened the door.

My knees buckled when I saw my best friend, who happened to be my wife, laying there, the picture of peace. Nothing could have prepared me for what followed. Her head was turned to the side and her mouth was crooked. It looked like she was biting her bottom lip. Beautiful but gone. I stood at her bedside and braced for the cold touch I knew was coming. My hope of waking up from the nightmare was extinguished when I touched her arm. I pulled the chair next to her bed and sat down. I hung my head and noticed tears on the floor from when our middle son had said his goodbyes earlier that night.

Breathe. Focus. Be Present.

I laid my head on her stomach with one arm across her chest. The other hand was free to wipe the tears coming from my eyes. I had no words. I was numb yet present, sad yet relieved for her suffering to be over. I spent much of the week studying her features so they would never leave my memory. Her eyes were amazing. She could just look at me and I knew everything would be alright, even if it wasn't. Selfishly, I wished I could have shared one last deep look into those green eyes.

My world was off its axis. I kissed her on the forehead and ran my fingers through her hair one last time while my tears fell on her cheeks. Breathe was the only thing happening. Focus was too painful, and I was done being present in this hell.

I passed the security guard as I left for what was now only my home. His "have a good day" parting words made me laugh for a moment. It was still dark when I returned to the house. Our son later told me I came in and went right to bed. The next morning, I woke up to my ex-husband, his wife, and stepdaughter knocking on the door. They offered their heartfelt sympathy and left an hour later. The kids were still at the house and we meandered all afternoon. What is it called when the auto pilot goes on auto pilot? Whatever the word, that was us.

The first task was ridding the pantry and refrigerator of the foods only she liked. Yeah. I know. What the hell? She was gone. It was the least upsetting place to begin and seemed like a logical place to start. One of my great joys in life was cooking for us. For her. She loved everything I made. We preferred cooking at home to going out for a meal. Our meals were sacred. After she died, food was the last thing on my mind. Yes, the grief helped fuel my aversion to eating but cooking was a constant reminder of her absence.

In the days immediately following her death, questions without answers blocked my thinking. Who would take care of me when I did not feel well? Tell me to breathe when I was crying? Hold my hand while I fell asleep? Take off my glasses when I fell asleep in bed? Remind me to eat? I wondered when the wanting to puke feeling would stop and how I would ever feel anything but sadness again. Blue told me that would take a minute.

One day I grabbed a piece of paper and wrote down a list of things I was learning about myself in this dead space.

*The first was that I needed to be more like my wife.

I was approached by a man in the parking lot of the grocery store on my first outing after she died. I stopped briefly to allow a large van to back out. As I continued toward my car the man offered some unsolicited advice. He said "Always watch out for cars in parking lots and cross sections. Those are the two most dangerous places for pedestrians." I thanked him and noticed he was wearing a teal blue t-shirt with a rainbow on it. Upon further examination I noticed it was an autism awareness graphic.

After I thanked him, he asked me if he could trouble me for $1.40 because he was hungry. I said, "I'm sorry, I didn't." I began to walk away, and he said, "I love you." I stopped in my tracks and remembered the cash in my purse from closing a small bank account earlier in the week.

Breathe. Focus. Be Present.

Flashes of my wife floated across my mind. She was the consummate giver, and, in that moment, I called out to him to wait. I walked toward him and handed him a five-dollar bill and told him to stay safe. In the fog of the week's events I just happened to pay attention.

On any other day I may have dismissed the encounter as just another meeting with any number of local panhandlers. On any other day my wife saw something different. Someone in need was someone in need.

Within our circle of friends and family she was known as the bleeding heart. While on a trip to Chicago for her sister's graduation from the University of Chicago we visited the Magnificent Mile. We encountered a blind man in a restaurant and later saw him on a corner. My friend and I told her he was not on the up and up.

My wife always saw an opportunity to offer whatever help she could give. She even gave her spare change to a man who scared the ever-living shit out of her by coming up on her as she loaded her car in a parking lot. She gave him a good talking to about the dangers of sneaking up on people like that, especially women, but she still helped him.

It did not matter what the person was going to do with the spontaneous donation. She gave because she felt like the act of giving was the important part. The rest of us cynics would lecture her and caution her to scrutinize the situation more closely before reaching in her purse to grab her change or loose bills. She would have none of it.

The second item came after this encounter with the stranger in the parking lot.

*Helping people is one way to handle change and deal with sadness.

The third item was:

*Be grateful for the blessing of knowing and experiencing real love.

It was a short list, but it meant everything to me. In order to move through this season of life, I needed to discover who I was without her and start the process of moving forward, and through the unknown. My authenticity took a left hook to the jaw November 26th, 2017. Could I practice what I preached?

3 - BECOMING AUTHENTIC

Authenticity was important to Yvette. So much so she spent the last few years of her life doing the work and learning to embrace who she was while understanding where she had been throughout her life. After she died, I found a journal in one of her dresser drawers. She was not a fan of writing anything down, especially thoughts and feelings. It took weeks to bring myself to open it up and read it. The pages contained proof of the hamster wheel that was her brain. A testament to what moving through truly looks like.

Her struggle was real, raw, and brutally honest. I am sure she never thought another soul would see it. Within the pages of that journal were jarring glimpses of her conflicted mind but also wisdom and determination. Her self-reflection included strong statements of hope as she handled her shit. The page where she named the beliefs, feelings, and rules she operated most of her life under was startling. I knew her better than anyone. How she saw herself was not how I, or anyone else, viewed her. Her life was not easy. She was strong. And stubborn. Both qualities served her well, but she struggled mightily to find peace with herself.

Her beliefs were rooted in her past. Most of ours are. The feelings which resulted from those beliefs included anxiety, fear, sadness, stress, and inadequacy. As she moved through life, she created a skewed set of rules for operating in the world. Keep your distance. Stay aloof. Go out of your way for others so they won't leave. Never show your true feelings because people will abandon you. Find out what you did wrong. Fix things at your own expense. Be skinny. Sound familiar?

Her authenticity was stifled early on. The space and permission to be herself happened after leaving her first marriage. She fought it and was certain the bottom was going to fall out from under her, and us, at any moment. It was a struggle to convince her I was not going anywhere. I kept telling her how I saw her was not how she saw herself. My words did little to stop the skipping record in her mind playing the song of her distorted beliefs, feelings, and rules.

Coming out was a huge victory in authentic living for her. Her Moving Through project told the story of her life. For the first time she allowed something to be about her. She spoke of the things that, up until she got diagnosed with cancer, she could not speak. She was fearless but still bogged down with her past.

Her life story is a blueprint for overcoming the things that suffocate authenticity in our lives. Her life covered all the bases. Some common things which suffocate authenticity in our lives include religion, other people's opinions, unhealthy relationships, low self-esteem, fear, emotional or physical trauma, upbringing, addiction, and negativity.

Through determination and encouragement, the path her life took did not destroy her. When she died, the story of her life was not one of despair but rather one of perseverance. As a photographer, she worked through her demons from behind the lens of a camera. She was an optimist and always believed peace was possible.

As a young child she was precocious and talkative. My words, not hers. She would have said she was a pain in the ass and always in trouble. Although her road was filled with mental and physical abuse, she always had hope. Her quest for authenticity was lifelong. The ghosts of her past were just as stubborn as she was. In our seven-year relationship I had front row seats to the process of her becoming more authentic. She finally began to realize the power inherent in shaking off the past.

Authenticity is not a destination, but rather a way of being which honors ourselves above all else. "Becoming" gay was not my first step toward being authentic. Had I had not understood authenticity, I never would have had the courage to come out as a lesbian. Which comes first? The chicken or the egg? My authentic journey began long before I even know I was gay. The journey along the road to authenticity is different for everyone. No one arrives at the same place at the same time.

The act of searching for something must begin with a plan of action. Accomplishing the goal of living authentically includes putting an end to distracting ourselves with busy work in order to discover our unique purpose. Easy enough, right? If only! In order to be authentic, one must understand what authenticity means. The definition of authentic is being true to one's own personality, spirit, or character; is sincere and authentic with no pretensions. In simple terms, being authentic is not letting other people determine what you do or how you feel about yourself. Authenticity is being comfortable with who you are and having the courage to choose your own path in life.

For me, it required an acceptance of the fact that I was okay, exactly as I was, on any given day. It meant accepting that my worth and value was not based on anything I said or did or any role that I played. Being yourself is not a new concept nor is it an unattainable goal. Ideally, the beauty of authenticity is found in the eyes of the beholder. Realistically, it is more complicated than that.

No one is born with low self-esteem or a distorted sense of who they are. Physiologically, the brain is shiny and new at birth. What gets in the way of living authentically? Where does the train go off the tracks? The answer to these questions is different for everyone.

My quest for authenticity manifested itself in a variety of ways throughout my whole life. A hallmark trait of inauthentic people is fear. Fear stops us from venturing below the surface to uncover what lies beneath.

Brutal honesty can be heartbreaking and painful. However, the act of seeking our own truth is what we are called to do. In order to live a truly authentic life you must discover who you are, what is important, and live accordingly. Being authentic and living authentically are one in the same.

If you whittle away at the stick long enough you will arrive at a point. It may not be easy, but it is simple. In order to be who you are you must embrace every experience and evaluate the impact each has had along the way. It is a matter of making up your mind over and repeatedly to choose peace. Brace yourself. The path of authenticity demands accepting every strength and weakness found within and choosing to let go of what was and embrace everything that is.

Tall order, right? On a good day this might be possible. However, if you are working from any deficit it is impossible. It is no secret that we all have baggage to deal with in our lives which affects our ability to live authentically. Being authentic is not a one and done concept. It is a continual process of choosing to honor your inner self regardless of the circumstances. Simple if you are a tree, but complicated if you are a human being.

The first 40 years of my life were filled with self-doubt, self-loathing, and layers of internal chaos caused by several factors. My conviction about the value and necessity of authentic living happened after I came out as a lesbian. "Be yourself" was the lesson. In my case it came at a great cost. A lifetime of questioning, searching, and reconciling elements of my past was the reward.

As you discover your authentic self, be prepared to deal with old messages and beliefs which have evolved over the years. Expect layers. Many layers. Getting to the center of the Tootsie Pop sometimes take more than three licks. Learning to be comfortable in our own skin is our mission. Embracing our true selves is our journey. Living authentically is our purpose. Give yourself and others permission to be who they are.

Take a moment to look beyond the awkward photos and focus on the image you have of who you know yourself to be. This is your authentic self. Whether it is wearing a dress, a suit, or is butt ass naked is not important. What is important is moving through the fear toward the life you were created for and to proudly own your unique place in the world.

Finding your true center is not a multiple-choice test and takes time, courage, and a willingness to be kind, patient, and loving with yourself. In this test there are no wrong answers. Dress how you want, love who you want, and be who you are without apology.

One of the most complimentary ways to describe someone is by saying they are genuine or down to earth. Genuine people are not free from baggage or flaws and find no reason to pretend to be anything other than who they are. How many truly genuine people are in your life? Would others define you as such? Good questions. Down to earth people have no problem matching their words with their actions.

We are all works in progress and the less phony people appear the more centered and grounded they truly are. These are the people that I gravitate towards. Does anyone enjoy spending time in the company of a phony person? Phoniness is a telltale sign there is a cover up going on. Hello insecurity.

Becoming Authentic

Insecurity encourages people to behave in ways which are contrary to what is going on beneath the surface. Behavior is frequently influenced by our internal dialogue, feelings, and emotions. Fear, anger, sadness, and joy are all major players in this game. Authenticity requires looking deeper than surface level. For many this is a strenuous task. Choosing to stay in the shallow end of the pool feels safe and offers some sense of control. Real transformation and peace happen in the deep end.

Seeking out the truth that lies beneath all our surfaces is not for the faint of heart. It is ugly at times and painful beyond belief other times. The act of seeking our own truth is in fact what we are called to do. This idea does not include those who operate most of the time under the umbrella of their own version of the truth. Remember, authenticity lacks excuse making and blaming others for our issues or emotional reactions.

Why did it take so long for me to finally get it? I did many things to help heal whatever was broken in me. Therapy, religion, hypnosis, moral inventory, and support groups just to name a few. The constant search for the one thing which would unchain my mind was exhausting. Exhaustion is an unavoidable part of the journey. After Yvette died, I was mentally, emotionally, and physically exhausted and peace was absent.

Authenticity is peace. Simple, right? So why do so many struggle to feel, experience, and live authentically? There are a million reasons why people struggle to be themselves, love who they are, and feel peace within. In order to figure out who we are, we first must examine the reasons why the struggle exists. Asking the right questions is a great place to begin.

4 - ASKING THE RIGHT QUESTIONS

Do you remember your first time? No, not that one. The moment when you felt like you had to adjust who you were in order to be accepted. Was it when you chose to shrink down and believe you were broken? Did it happen at home? At school? At church? While out playing with your friends? At the breakfast or dinner table? Was it a slow process or did something change in an instant?

Trying to pinpoint the moment when fear, insecurity, and negative self-talk began is a good starting point, however it may not bring answers. Some questions have no answers. If you are not sure, you are in good company. Understanding when it began is one step on the stairway to authenticity. Fact finding missions begin with the art of asking the right questions.

In middle school I learned the importance of asking the right questions from a remarkable journalism teacher. In her advisory role as the editor of the school newspaper she drilled home the necessity of fact checking articles before publication as well as keeping opinions out of our stories. I would not be shocked if trying to teach journalistic integrity and proper writing to a bunch of eager, obnoxious, and know it all seventh and eighth graders drove her to drink.

Asking who, what, why, when, and where covers the basics and helps clarify the facts, as well as give context to a situation. The additional question of "how," is also frequently included in this list. The final work should have a reader feeling like they were there for the actual event. These guidelines were my rules for writing about the school sports scene. Gathering facts and presenting an accurate account of what happened was the goal. Seemed simple enough.

My approach to adulthood has integrated the lessons learned from my time as a middle school sports reporter and provided insight, wisdom, and a framework for evaluating the path of my life. Profound, right? Growth and authenticity are the product of answering the questions which are unique to our life story. However, as life happens, arriving at the truth and living authentically can easily become convoluted.

Asking the right questions and an unbiased quest for the truth are not only hallmarks of solid journalism but also a healthy mind. Understanding the difference between facts and opinions is a cardinal principle of journalism. Other principles include independence, fairness and impartiality, humanity, and accountability. These concepts have a variety of applications. As the writers of our own lives, we can apply each of these principles and use them to define and live our truth.

Let's start with the ability to discern fact from opinion. Facts and opinions are often confused today. Facts are facts. A car is a car. The color of the car is another fact. How you feel about the color of the car is an opinion. My hair is gray and there are seven days in a week. More facts. Your feelings about those facts are opinions.

In a perfect world there would be a clear line differentiating fact and opinion. In the real world, the two are often confused. Understanding the difference is a critical aspect of authenticity. The truth about who we are, where we have been, and what is happening in our lives requires constant fact checking.

When writing, fact checking is paramount to producing accurate work. It requires long hours researching and verifying information before completing a story. The line between fact and fiction can be thin when our personal stories are examined.

Our perspective when it comes to judging our own stories is problematic. Stepping back and being able to see where the blurred lines have been is necessary for growth, but not a cake walk. Here is a lesson in perspective. Think back to your childhood home. My childhood home was a two-story colonial which always felt big. I was shocked to learn that the home was only 1300 square feet. My adult understanding of that size is more accurate than my opinion of how big it felt as a child. Leaving room for the possibility of inaccuracies in our perspective or truth helps pave the way for authenticity to flourish.

The ability to remain fair and impartial is another principle of good journalism. Most stories have at least two sides. While there is no obligation to present every side in every piece, stories should be balanced and add context. Objectivity is not always possible but impartial reporting builds trust and confidence. An unbiased piece is credible and allows room for the reader to form their own opinion about the work or story.

Maintaining an independent position about our lives is challenging. Remaining independent prevents outside influences seeping into the finished piece. Negative bias blocks impartiality and affects how we view the world, others, and most importantly ourselves. How often do we allow what other people think affect our finished product? How often is our negative mindset the cause of internal chaos and false conclusions?

The concept of humanity and accountability are the final two tenets. Humanity states that journalists should do no harm. Again, in a perfect world, every writer would be aware of the impact of their words and images on the lives of others. What about the effect our own words have on our inner selves?

Accountability is my favorite principle. Ask my children. It states that professional and responsible journalists can hold themselves accountable. Correcting errors and expressing sincere regret without cynicism is not a popular activity for most of us. It is the cynicism part which snags us. When was the last time you offered a sincere apology? Cynicism is a highly weaponized form of ego.

Accepting responsibility for our part in a situation, circumstance, or outcome requires maturity, honesty, and humility. Although unpleasant, learning to take our lumps and swallowing pride is a valuable part of the human experience.

The brief introduction to the principles of journalism may seem like I went off on a tangent. Humor me here and it might begin to make sense. What would happen if you followed these principles and wrote your own story according to them? How would shifting the view of our story affect our lives? If we began examining our story like the editor of a newspaper does an article, would we feel different?

Here is another question. What does any of this have to do with learning how to make peace with the past and live authentically? The answer is everything. In order to explain how to find peace and embrace authentic living, the blocks to authenticity must be recognized, evaluated, addressed, and understood.

Before we begin, identifying and understanding the contributing factors from the past which influenced our body of work must happen. The individual chapters in our personal lives tell our story. As is true with most novels, there are antagonists, plot twists, and a myriad of colorful characters which appear on the pages of our lives. Some chapters are light, and others may be dark. Both are equally important and influence our behavior and mindset.

Learning how to identify, reconcile, and answer the questions of who, what, when, where, and how our true selves became suffocated or buried is the first step in discovering how to live authentically. The individual plots and players may vary for us all, but the journey is eerily similar. No one has the luxury of living life in a vacuum. We share threads in an intricately woven quilt. Our individual swatches were created from a lifetime of experiences, colored by messages received, and comprised of interactions with family, friends, and even strangers.

The preliminary laundry list of things which squash and impede us from accepting ourselves wholly is lengthy. Emotional or physical trauma, low self-esteem, fear, religion, unhealthy relationships, addiction, or societal expectations are a few of the more prevalent players.

Let's start at the very beginning. It's a very good place to start. No, it does not begin with Do Re Mi, but rather those pesky elephants in the rooms of the past. Yes. It all started there. Warning alert about taking extended unguided journeys in the way back machine: don't go alone. Reflection is good but exercise caution about staying there too long. Remember the goal of going back is clarity, not confusion.

Often, digging up old dirt spreads dust everywhere. Mapping out the exact moment when you felt like you had to adjust or sacrifice who you were in order to be accepted is complicated. Humans are notorious for running from discomfort and pain, forgetting healing and growth only happen in this uncomfortable space. The dustbowl is a vessel for peace. Standing firmly and waiting for the debris to settle reveals the truth. If you are willing to pick through the debris, organize the mess, and reorder the piles from the past, the freedom to change the narrative of your life will follow.

5 - ROADBLOCKS TO AUTHENTICITY

I have read hundreds of self-help books and listened to countless discussions about how to be your best self, find peace, and live authentically. Knowledge is power, right? Parsing through the theories, action plans, explanations, and opinions can bring more confusion and questions. If you are like me, being inundated with solutions can be intimidating. Which plan should I follow? Whose advice is the best? What should I do? Can someone please just tell me what to do!

Information overload can backfire. I walked away from many books and seminars feeling worse than when I started. Instead of feeling encouraged and motivated, I felt defeated and incapable of executing the wisdom suggested by the author or speaker. The reminder of the amount of work I had yet to accomplish, paired with my own self-doubt, was a blue-ribbon winning recipe for staying stuck.

Roadblocks to authenticity begin early in life. Figuring out your authentic self requires the freedom to express yourself. Emotional or physical trauma, low self-esteem, fear, religion, anxiety and depression, unhealthy relationships, addiction, or societal expectations are some roadblocks to authenticity.

Remember, authenticity is a peace about who we are and the ability to navigate life without concern for what other people think, while remaining committed to living our own personal truth, despite outside opinion. It requires a deep sense of self and a willingness to own every flaw and moment of poor decision making in the past. It strips away the victim suit and creates a sense of humility and understanding about how actions can affect others. In order to be truly authentic, you must own and subsequently become skilled at handling your shit.

When the deck is stacked it is hard to win a hand at the table. It just takes one moment of clarity, and sometimes luck, to win a hand. Figuring out how to be comfortable, confident, and content with yourself takes time. For some of us the deck is stacked. No one is immune from chaos or has figured out a way to shield themselves from the impact our past can have on our lives. If the goal of being authentic includes accepting of every aspect of yourself, even the ugly parts, and living your life without allowing any other person, place, or thing to alter your path, how do we get there?

I wondered why things had to be so complicated and could not help feeling like there should be an easier way to feel better. Looking for the fix was a distraction and nothing more than busy work which kept taking me around the same mountain repeatedly. Sound familiar?

Roadblocks to Authenticity

The quest to find the one thing that solves the mystery of a peace filled life is a common activity. Lean in, I have a secret to share. The one moment when everything is good, and all is right with the world does not exist. A magic pill which guarantees peace has not been discovered. Looking for a tried and true method which will remedy inner conflict and unlock the door to nirvana is another trip around the mountain. The desire to fix ourselves is the first item on the grocery list, but should it be?

Believing we can "fix" ourselves is flawed thinking and sets us up for failure right out of the gate. We are not cars with flat tires that need repairing. It is not that easy, but it is simple if you begin to embrace the idea that there will never be one moment in our lives when everything is "fixed."

WAYBACK MACHINE

Time to walk the walk. My struggle to embrace my authenticity was lengthy and ugly. I woke up every day fighting to keep myself together. I did not eat or sleep well for many years. The anxiety running rampant in my life was suffocating. In order to deal with my emotions, I needed to step back. Opening the vault and looking at my childhood through adult eyes was trying.

One day, a therapist asked me to describe my childhood. Crickets. The usual "it was okay" answer did not fly. Seeing my discomfort and deer in the headlights look prompted a follow up question. "Were you happy as a child?" How ridiculous. What I wanted to say was "If I was, would I be sitting here in this office?" but what came out of my mouth was "no." Surprised by my own answer, I began to panic and offer a clever rationalization for what just slipped out of my mouth.

Admitting out loud that my seemingly okay childhood was unhappy broke the unspoken code of silence within my family. Back track. Repair. Explain. My childhood included a home, food to eat, and clothes. There were no regular beatings or serious crises to contend with. How could I say that my childhood was unhappy when I was provided the physical necessities? Plenty had far worse and there was no way to justify any complaints I had.

Taking the "it could have been worse" approach was a defense mechanism which protected me from going down the rabbit hole. In high school, an English teacher asked me if there was anything going on at home I needed to talk about. Apparently, I was not very stealthy and my creative writing assignments gave her cause to inquire. Nope. She was not convinced and referred me to the school counselor. The very brief meeting included her asking the same and me responding with one-word answers.

Minimizing the impact of years of living in a home where fear and avoidance were present was the name of the game. Learning from the therapist that my feelings mattered changed everything. Getting permission to explore and investigate the impact of growing up in an inconsistent environment was the beginning of healing.

As a child, I was full of self-doubt, afraid and very anxious. These feelings came out in many forms over the years. Children absorb their environments and learn how to behave accordingly. My family members did not deal with one another in a healthy way. We did not have family meetings or constructive conversations. We did our own thing, ate dinner together, and went our own ways. The rules were arbitrary and random depending on the day. The fear of what could happen to me limited my freedom and created more anxiety within.

As the oldest of three children, I was the most sheltered and often felt controlled and angry. My mom's fear of something happening to me out in the world made me question my trustworthiness. I became a giant pain in the ass. My mouth was legendary.

When you are in a dysfunctional home, how you view yourself is affected. Stipulation. People do what they know. A family is only as healthy as the weakest link. The first social group in life is the family. How a family operates as a unit is determined by the ability of the individuals to handle their shit. Some are better than others. Mine was no different. Families are human.

The underlying belief in my life was that I was not important and did not matter. No biggie, right? Where the feeling comes from is only the first step on the ladder. The root is far less important than figuring out how to move past the thinking. Getting laughed at for being afraid or for crying helped fuel the engine. I was teased for being a tomboy. I carried this feeling for years. I felt stupid and different.

The feelings created an internal dialogue of unimportance. My worst trigger over the years is this specific demon. When I feel unimportant, my best defense mechanisms jump into action. Worth noting is that I cannot remember someone flat out telling me I did not matter or that I was not important. I learned early that watching what people did carried more weight than what they said. My perception was flawed but valid.

YOU CAN RUN BUT YOU CAN'T HIDE

The realization that our past provides fuel for our present sucks. Kids are experts at adapting to their environment and finding a workaround to the mental and emotional disappointments experienced. The problem is when we become adults, these things follow us and many times we do not even realize their effect on our behavior and choices. My workaround during my teen years was being sneaky. It was my way of ensuring some of the activities I knew would be squashed if I was forthcoming could happen.

At 18, I thought living away from home would help remedy the immediate stress. After all, I was still bitter about moving from Michigan to Florida during the middle of my junior year in high school. I discovered years later that this move made just as little sense to most in my extended family as it did to me. Even though I was away at school, I took all the self-loathing and self-destructive ways with me.

The day I left for college, I packed my clothes, my personal belongings, and the effects of living with my own brand of anxiety into the car. I brought along my declaration of rebellion which was born out of the injustice of relocating me and entered dorm life. This was an exciting time, however I realized I was not emotionally or mentally prepared for the trip. Stuffed emotions always find a way out eventually. The ghosts that followed were present in every relationship and contaminated everything I touched.

I took full advantage of my self-destructive powers during the first couple of years I was out from under the perceived regime of tyranny. I did not imagine this new phase of my life would teeter so close to the edge of darkness at times. When you combine a taste of freedom with a very low self-image then the fun begins.

I chose to drink as my own escape and in doing so I managed to rid myself of any sense of dignity or self-worth by acting out in every way possible. Late night benders and missing classes was the rule and not the exception. Convincing myself distance would bring relief from the lack of freedom and family dynamic was easy. I was not sure what I was looking for but knew being away from home would help.

Running was the ultimate avoidance tactic. However, I was terrified. I was wandering aimlessly and wondered who would be the first to realize that this loud-mouthed rude chick was really a mess on the inside. My first semester was a blur as I spent many nights drunk and being obnoxious. Self-medicating is not something I recommend. Additionally, I blew off work study responsibilities which resulted in my parents coughing up a decent chunk of change at the end of the semester. Ouch.

Despite my "going away for the first time" growing pains, the year ended much better than it began. A few days before freshman year ended, I could feel the protective shield go up in preparation for being back at home. There was little evidence to support that when

I went home, I would be treated any differently than before I left. Going off to college did not change the environment that was waiting for me when I returned.

There was a palpable tension. I was 18 years old and felt the leash go back around my neck the instant I walked in the door. It was going to be a long summer. I began to discover how to live on my own in the insulated world of the university setting. I was selected to be a resident advisor for the upcoming school year, which was something I was extremely proud of accomplishing.

Being a part of the residential life staff was a step in the right direction. The goal of figuring out who I was and what I was good at doing was a win for team progress. I made great friends and lost a small piece of the chip on my shoulder I arrived with.

I returned home and was hired to work for Florida Power and Light as a switchboard operator. It was my first full time job. Adjusting to life back at home was frustrating because the freedom I was accustomed to while away was gone. Despite being 18 going on 19, I once again found myself asking permission to go anywhere. Every inch of freedom was a fight. The arguments got very heated at times. I was tired of being treated like a child and reporting my every move. It was suffocating and exhausting.

IN THE DARK

Feeling defeated sent me to a dark place. I was so unhappy that summer. As July approached, I reached a low point. In a moment of complete hopelessness, I decided enough was enough. This was the first time I considered suicide. In a final act of desperation, I called a close friend and shared my darkness. Reaching out was my last resort. Instead of ending my life, I listened to her. Her words shed some light on the darkness I was feeling. Ironically, it was July 4th.

Her words helped renew my sense of determination and ability to wait out returning to school a few weeks later. I was living day by day and clinging to the fact that I would be out of the weeds in a month so. I thought this bout of darkness was behind me when I began my sophomore year but would find out a few months later there were lingering feelings to deal with. Willing life to be different and experiencing a true change in outlook and mindset are not the same thing. I was good at ordering and locking away my feelings. I still lacked the skills to deal with my demons in a healthy way.

The second time I considered suicide was during the fall of my sophomore year. Again, I felt off. I was in what would become the most destructive relationship of my life. This guy was a mess too. We enjoyed being a mess together. Misery loved company, but we made it look fun. One night we got pulled over after dollar pitcher long island iced tea night. Yeah. Stellar move. He was driving below the speed limit. To this day I have no idea how he was not arrested for DUI. Somehow he managed to leave with a warning. Despite the "fun," I was struggling. The toxic relationship was a symptom of what was going on with me. Once again, I decided my feelings and darkness were too much to deal with.

I was lost, confused, angry, and scared but most of all, hopeless. This time my decision to let on that I was again feeling suicidal resulted in residential life staff becoming involved. In hindsight, I do not think I would have followed through but the attention I was seeking backfired on me. I was turned in by the same friend that I had confided in during the past summer. Twice is a pattern in case you are wondering. I would have done the same thing had I been in her shoes. Even though sober adult Dawn knows it was the right thing to do, when it went down, I was pissed off.

As a result of my actions, I was given two options. Go to a psychiatrist to be evaluated and be allowed to stay in school or get sent home. I was angry but thought it laughable that the plan to send me home was on the table. Just ridiculous. How I felt, the roots of the feelings, and the circumstances which created the mess were known to those offering the choices. I questioned how option two would help alleviate the mental slop pile, so I chose counseling. My parents were called, updated, set up the appointment, and arranged for the payment. I could stay. Side note: since then, no words have been spoken about this by any of us.

For three months I saw the psychiatrist. I was prescribed an antidepressant and eventually came to the realization that letting my past control me was self-destructive. The therapist gave me some rudimentary tools to help with my anxiety and negative thinking and I graduated from the mandated course of care. Although I fought the process, it did help tremendously. I was able to speak freely and receive validation about my feelings. I came away from that experience feeling more grounded than I had felt in a long time.

One of the conditions for me remaining in school was seeing the school counselor on a weekly basis. Poor Judy. I was closed off, angry, and outright defiant at the onset of the sessions. I knew just how far I could go before I was over the line. I pushed it frequently. My attendance was not voluntary, so I dug in my heels and was a royal pain in the ass. Although I was resistant, I did manage to absorb the lesson of let go or be dragged. Realizing the process was meant to help me, I dropped my bullshit and guard and began to do the work. My behavior was a symptom of my stuck mindset. I had choices to make and the freedom to decide how I was going to move through my life. The process challenged my angry, not enough, and unimportant internal dialogue.

One of my hang ups was being touched by people. I was never a hugger and guarded myself at all costs from this type of interaction. I was too raw at the time to let people in. After every session, Judy asked me for a hug. The first few weeks I laughed in her face and stood my ground. I was a jerk and not a model client. Her patience and ability to help me reframe my past helped me change my flawed thinking. I left therapy with an attitude of gratitude and a new perspective on life.

For however enlightened I felt after making progress in therapy, I still struggled with figuring out who I was. I was twenty years old and wanted an immediate answer. I thought that college was the time and place when you worked out the kinks and became a real adult person. Discovering your path in life came with the diploma. I was working out some kinks, but it felt more like putting out fires than self-actualization. Side note: The process of healing takes more than a few visits to a shrink and is a process which takes years to happen.

Moving Through

This was simply the beginning of my evolution. In the meantime, I was still inundated with feelings of unworthiness and guilt. The burden of my past choices was hard to shake. Unsure of how to let go and forgive myself for the things I did that I was not proud of, I became stuck. Round the mountain we go. The decision to view myself as damaged and not important led me to abuse my body, spirit, and mind. On multiple occasions.

Despite the struggle, not everything was a mess. I graduated with a bachelor's degree and married my college sweetheart. We started a life together which helped quiet my negative mindset. Life was happening and I was happily along for the ride. Enter motherhood.

My path took a detour when I began my own family. Shit got real then. A healthy family dynamic was my goal. I had work to do. The negative mindset crept in again. My plan for keeping it together was to be tough and closed off. An impossible task for someone with a husband and children. My feelings of superiority interfered with my humility. Judging others for their choices was a way for me to feel better about my own past mistakes. I really thought I had my shit together. I set myself up as the one with the great life and took on the job of family consigliere. I provided guidance and was convinced my way was right and would fix any problem. I was the go-to gal. I felt important.

I was strong and athletic, bold, and tough. My source of confidence was shaky and created issues up and down the pike. My high horse took off without me when I realized inserting myself into others' lives was a way to avoid facing my own fears about parenting, marriage, and being good enough. In order to be authentic, I could not skip past my issues with self-control, self-loathing, resentments, and expectations. I resented not having freedom and created unrealistic expectations for those in my life. My angry words and harsh exterior kept the self-loathing in the foreground.

Despite a valiant effort to keep a present-moment mindset, my programming led my brain to either jump ahead or look back. Hello anxiety. My plan to compartmentalize emotions affected the relationships with my husband and children, and more importantly, with myself. I wondered if I could ever deprogram and reconfigure my circuit board. My life-long habit of letting anxiety rule the roost caught up with me and I had a decision to make.

The belief that feelings were an enemy served me for a time. Through the love of my friends, other family members, and husband, I was able to dismantle my protective walls. The process took years to unfold. There was much work to be done in the areas of forgiveness, healing, and personal growth. Understanding the past opened the door to healing and provided the clarity to let go of the habits which were no longer helpful.

6 - UNDERSTANDING THE PAST

Avoiding hunting down and facing your childhood demons is harmful to not only your children, but yourself. It was not until I became a parent that I got serious about healing my past. Despite every best intention, parents make mistakes which can impact their children on a cellular level. Humans are not perfect. Parents are human. Perfection is an unattainable goal and the push for perfect families and lives has created more problems than solutions.

Upbringing plays an important role in determining an individual's narrative. There is a reason why therapists choose to ask about childhood at the onset of therapy. In theory, the goal of therapy is to evaluate what happened, not to fix the past. How and why are not as important as what. The information revealed after the curtain is pulled back is crucial to understanding the plot.

How someone is raised is more than just being taught right from wrong, how to be polite, or treat others. The story of our life has

Understanding the Past

many contributing authors. Parents are the creators and first contributors to the body of work that is our life.

Learning how to move past the ingrained messages and create peace is the goal. Many are not aware of the power to write the script of their own lives and feel powerless to change the dialogue, especially when seeds from the past have stubborn roots.

Our beginnings are only a small part of the book, but the early chapters often set the tone and mood for moving through life. A child who grew up in a comprised environment often becomes an adult who is prone to continue the cycle of dysfunction. Dysfunction comes in many forms. Some obvious, others hidden. Trauma, addiction, and abuse are obvious forms of dysfunction. Hidden dysfunction can include silent contracts or emotionally unhealthy relationships fueled by fear or a need to control. Children who are not nurtured in a healthy way feel the effects for a lifetime.

Upbringing is defined as the treatment and instruction received by a child from their parents throughout childhood. Seems self-explanatory. Training is an accurate synonym as well. How someone is brought up can be influenced by cultural, religious, geographical, and socioeconomic factors. The environment children are raised in plays a critical role in the formation of healthy thinking and self-esteem.

Even those with the most idyllic of childhoods can emerge feeling broken. Events happen which can leave long lasting marks in the skin. Losing a parent or belonging to a family where secrets are the norm have the potential to leave scars. Whether accidental, intentional, or because it was a day ending with the letter Y, no one escapes childhood unscathed. As bleak as this sounds, within each of us lies the power to heal the past and break the chains of chaos. The natural ebb and flow include both amazing and devastating moments.

The intent of a parent is worth consideration but what seeps in is often unexpected. The intent is less important than the impact of the message received. Messages can be inadvertently or intentionally shared. Teaching a child that second place is the first loser may seem like a positive message about working hard and striving for the best. Conversely, it could also convey the message that unless you win or come in first you have failed.

The nature versus nurture theory teaches that humans are products of both genetics and environment. Scientifically speaking, genotype is our genetic makeup while phenotype refers to the physical expression of that gene in our behavior. Your environment and your genes play a role in influencing the phenotype.

Our genetics are just one variable in the equation. Who we become is also formed by the physical, emotional, and mental environment we are raised in. How we interpret the world is filtered through the experiences, emotions, and circumstances surrounding life. The stream of information, stimuli, and energy we are exposed to shapes how we see the world and ourselves.

What sticks to us, whether it be rooted in thoughts, word, or deed, can be a crap shoot. The impact of the messages received can be positive, negative, or neutral and the impact will vary. How one person responds to something may not be how another responds. Using the above example, saying second place is the first loser may push one child to succeed, while the next child may give up.

Families are like little countries. Each family has its own set of rules and a culture that is fostered daily. If you grew up in a family where a parent was abusive or controlling, you may not know this to be a bad thing. It was what you knew, and it was normal. Same is true of those growing up in homes where emotional, physical, or sexual abuse, addiction, or neglect was present.

These circumstances bring a host of issues which seriously impact the ability to achieve emotional, mental, and spiritual health. Adding elements of abuse, addiction, or trauma of any kind creates a mountain to climb and brings about damage which some struggle with for a lifetime. Survival mode undermines authentic living.

Simply put, the environment someone is raised in plays an enormous role in determining the ease with which they progress through life. Difficulty yields difficulty. Ease yields ease. But not always. Our beginnings set the stage for what is to come. Unfortunately, children do not have the luxury of choosing the family they are born in to. Children are blank slates and are famous for being unpredictable, sponge-like creatures who absorb and take in everything they are exposed to. Good and bad.

What follows is prefaced by the stipulation that parents are not perfect. Some are better suited to the job than others. Anyone can have a baby. Even the most conscientious parent makes mistakes and can inadvertently pass along unhealthy messages to their children during key moments in their development. There is no better way to see one's faults and weakness than to have children. For me, I was forced to take responsibility for the baggage I carried, acknowledge the things which were not working, and start to seriously address the blips in my own thinking. Being a parent is more than just babysitting.

Raising another person is a huge responsibility. However, parents often fail to recognize the responsibility to make sure that they themselves are healthy. Plain and simple, screwed up people create screwed up children. Better yet, dysfunctional people raise dysfunctional people. The slow decline of our voice, power, or self-worth began somewhere. Examining the past sheds light on the inability to live life on their own terms, without apology, hesitation, or shame.

When stressed or in a state of mental unrest, people tend to devote their energy to searching for answers in the wrong places. Especially about the past. Taking another trip down journalism road for a minute. The question of who, what, where and when are easy to determine. Answering the questions of "why" and "how" often become the focus. Finding the connection between the events of the past and negative thinking can be an unpleasant journey.

Does anyone enjoy the emotional exercise of ripping open old wounds or revisiting painful moments in life? Looking for answers or explanations is a fantastic way to unearth even more dirt which must be addressed. In hindsight, the temptation to focus on the "how" is strong. How could such and such have happened?

Understanding the Past

Questioning in this way implies responsibility for the outcome. If we could figure out how, the chance for a solution should increase.

The kissing cousin to "how," is "why." Why did such and such happen? Why did they do such and such? Why didn't I such and such? Sound familiar? Focusing on how does not always answer the question why. Knowing why does not change what may have happened nor does it stop the emotions, feelings, or thoughts from swirling. My diagnosis of Generalized Anxiety Disorder was the how for me but answering why is impossible. The desire to control the uncontrollable is at the core of the questioning process.

However, getting caught up in the questions diverts attention from the matter at hand. Dwelling on questions distracts us from the big picture and peace. The downward spiral is a direct result of spending too much time dwelling on what was instead of focusing on what is. Being able to view the past in its proper context allows freedom to move forward. Focusing on what is opens the vault to healing.

Allowing the wounds of the past to heal is a heavy task. Questioning the wisdom of a universe which allows children to be born into dangerous, unhealthy, and dysfunctional families is common. Resisting the urge to keep picking at the scabs requires discipline and accepting some questions do not have answers.

Lingering damage appears in all areas of life. Making peace with the past often requires resurrecting painful memories, emotions, and the events from childhood. Addressing the past is one way to understand the present.

Moving Through

BAGGAGE

Identifying lingering ghosts or messages affecting self-image is a good place to start. It took many years to know, understand, and like who I am. It took years to acknowledge the toll dysfunctional environments had but helped illuminate the source of my flawed thinking later in life. Understanding the far-reaching impact of my upbringing was the first step toward healing and moving forward.

In order to unpack accumulated baggage every suitcase and piece of clothing must be scrutinized, laundered, and folded neatly to be put away. Baggage comes in many shapes, colors, and sizes. Some have carry-on sized bags and others are traveling with numerous large suitcases. Three things are needed in order to successfully claim your baggage.

The first is recognition. When the conveyor belt starts moving you must know which bag belongs to you. Recognition is not always automatic. You cannot change what you do not recognize. My dad played professional baseball in Japan when I was a toddler. When my parents arrived in Japan, my dad's garment bag was missing. He waited for the bag to appear on the conveyor belt in baggage claim, but it was nowhere to be found. Not the best way to begin a new adventure. Later in the day, my mom mentioned seeing someone with a bag that looked like his walking past them. She did not recognize it was his and whatever was in the garment bag was gone forever. This small lapse in recognition made for an expensive shopping trip to replace the items lost.

Once the luggage is recognized, the next step is picking it up and placing it in the car. The heavier the suitcase, the harder it is to move. However, if we do not recognize our baggage, there is nothing to put it in the car. During the dark days, my baggage was camouflaged and hard to recognize. My vision was obscured by self-loathing and fear. Although I tripped over it every day, I was resistant to shift my gaze downward and truly unpack the load.

The second is awareness. Being aware of who was involved with the packing process helps explain the weight of the cargo and the source. The third thing necessary is strength. Both physical and mental.

Heavy lifting requires strong muscles and a determined mindset. Recognition, awareness, and strength are simple concepts when talking about literal baggage. Figurative baggage is a completely different animal and brings us back to the discussion of how upbringing influences how we think, behave, and feel about the world and ourselves.

CHAOS

Internal chaos affects everything. Negativity is a sure-fire indicator of the presence of chaos and is the ultimate killer of peace. Examples of this can be found every time we leave the house, turn on the television, or interact with people. As a rule, internal chaos creates external chaos. When internal chaos is running the show, it is nearly impossible to achieve anything closely resembling peace in our lives. Internal chaos is not a crazy calendar filled with appointments and jobs to do. It is the thoughts and views we hold about ourselves and others which create feelings of inadequacy, defensiveness, and negative energy.

Every action or reaction we have passes through our internal filter before it is put out into the world. Healthy people do not create chaos in the world. Again, having children helped enlighten me. Making the decision to address my own chaos was easy when it became painfully clear that my chaos was their chaos. It took many years to get to the place where I am now. It did not happen overnight. It was intense and at times, a supreme pain in the ass. Choosing peace over chaos is challenging, especially when the outside world thrives on it.

Keeping peace in our lives may be a challenge, but it is not impossible. Working toward peace within requires much less energy than fighting the chaos, the world, or one another. There are many who do not believe they are entitled to peace. Life is messy and can be hard. Nothing breaks my heart more than seeing those who believe they are undeserving of love and a peace filled life. We are deserving of peace and in chaos we are still capable of creating it for ourselves. The first step is getting out of our own way and taking out the trash that litters our minds and hearts. I know. It is easier said than done. But do it anyway.

Creating peace within looks like deflecting messages which make us question our worth and value. It begins with turning the volume down and deciding to listen to a new genre of music. Changing how we think about ourselves is a decision that supports peace. Focusing on strengths instead of flaws is a great place to start.

Understanding the Past

We do not owe the world anything, but we owe ourselves everything. It comes down to this. If we all chose to deal with our internal chaos, the world would be better for it. This may mean dealing with guilt, self-esteem issues, the past, or just practicing the lost art of forgiveness. It may mean accepting who we are at our core and embracing it even though our friends and family may not be on the same page. We owe it to ourselves to do whatever we can to recognize the things in our lives that are stealing our potential for peace and to remember that peace and love can never fail.

SHAME AND GUILT

What is shame? Where does it come from? How can it be overcome? Is it possible to live authentically if you are bogged down with either? Understanding the nature of shame and how it presents itself in daily life is a complicated process.

Feelings of shame are something everyone can relate to. Our history, life experience, and view of ourselves provide fertile ground for shame. What can we do to change the filter through which we see ourselves so that shame can be sent packing?

Before we can answer that question, we must first define shame. Freedictionary.com says it is a painful emotion caused by the belief that one is, or is perceived by others to be, inferior or unworthy of affection or respect because of one's actions, thoughts, circumstances, or experiences.

Carl Jung refers to it as "a soul eating emotion", which is spot on. I define it as that little voice that screams, "I am not good enough, lovable, or acceptable because of who I am". It is the inherent belief that despite anything I may do, I feel bad about who I am. Shame also makes us shrink down and question our worthiness to exist.

Members of the gay community are well versed in the shame game. Refer to the inferior part of the definition above. Fighting shame is a common task for those in the LGBTQ community. For many of my gay brothers and sisters, religion is a common source of deep-seated shame thinking. Feeling like something is wrong with you is reinforced by families who refuse to accept "the lifestyle" and a society which is averse to anything other than the traditional. The coming out process is grueling because shame screams you are not normal.

Fears about being rejected by loved ones, or the world, create internal stress, agony, and shame about being different. Sharing it with the world blows out the speakers. The choice to be authentic and embrace who you are is challenging enough. Adding shame to the mix intensifies the situation. Shame comes in many forms and was a huge obstacle in Yvette's life. She was ashamed about her past and how she came to be.

Her mom married young and became pregnant soon after marrying. Her mother left her biological father when she 6 months old in order to be with her high school sweetheart. When she was two years old they married, and he adopted her soon after. When she was thirteen, she found out that the man she had known as her father was not her biological father. It was a huge secret in her family. Her mom treated her poorly, and was physically abusive to her, which made her feel like she was a mistake and a reminder of

Understanding the Past

the failed marriage between her mom and biological father. She never felt like she was loved without condition.

In her adult life her shame manifested itself by causing her to shrink down and feel like she was a mistake. She was always watching and reading the reactions of those around her. Yvette was a pro at blending into whatever situation she came upon. I was one of the few people who knew her story. I guessed something was off. She never actually told me on her own. Despite my assurances, she struggled to feel like her existence mattered. That belief colored her decisions and how she viewed her purpose in the world.

Shame chooses others over yourself because you feel unworthy of love or inferior. Shame blinds us from the possibility of redemption and creates the belief that no matter what we say or do, our unworthiness will prevail. Not good. So, what happens now?

In order to release shame-based thinking, you must investigate the source and begin creating a new internal dialogue. It is not easy and often painful, but it is possible. Abuse is notorious for creating shame in our lives. There is hope.

The best way to confront and eliminate shame is to expose the source. Once the source is identified you can begin to heal. Healing takes many forms and varies depending on the situation. Often shame creates feeling of powerlessness. Taking back power is the best way to combat it.

The night Yvette debuted her first show to a theater full of people, she chose the nuclear option for shame and guilt. "Moving Through" used dance, photography, and music to tell her emotional life story. As she spoke to the audience, I saw her hands shaking. She was terrified. Choosing to go deeper and share private details of her journey was the bravest thing I had ever seen. She held nothing back. While she gave the introduction, I stared at the floor up in the loft at the rear of the theater. I was emotional and so proud of her.

As she spoke, I watched the audience begin to respond. Rawness and honesty were front and center. Literally. She detailed her struggles with an eating disorder, body image, and low self-esteem. Speaking about the loss of the relationship with her son after coming out and leaving an emotionally abusive marriage resonated with many in attendance. Shame and guilt did not have tickets to this show. By the end of the show, many were in tears and later shared how deeply affected they were by her story. And courage. It was powerful and inspiring stuff folks.

Speaking out loud helped quiet the messages from her past, called out shame for what it was, and was a major step in her healing process. In that moment, the truth of who she is was clear. She landed a powerful blow to old thinking and cut some swatches out of the quilt of the past. Shame makes us shrink when we should stand tall and is a silencer. Truth is loud. Speaking truthfully and honestly lessens the grip and allows the light to flood in. Disrupting the circuit is one way to move through and decrease the shame dialogue.

Refusing to give weight to the flawed inner whispers shifts the power to its rightful place. To you. Going toe to toe with the old messages may seem like an uphill battle, but you are the general and have all the resources and inside intelligence within you to win the war. Waging a war on shame will bring freedom and go a long way to cultivate happiness and promote peace in life.

Sharing experiences and stories makes it possible to break the chains of fear and shame. Be brave and brutally honest. Spend time considering the impact they have on your life. Authenticity is possible when shame is kicked to the curb.

Simply put, the problem of shame relates to viewing our being as flawed. Along the way, unhealthy messages, false information, and negative life experiences are given priority and can eventually become our truth. Then comes guilt.

We experience feelings of guilt for a variety of reasons. Guilt is the cousin to shame, but not a sibling. Shame comes from who we think we are whereas guilt comes from the things we do, have done, or have failed to do.

This is the big kahuna for late in life lesbians, especially guilt over breaking up a family and the inevitable changes, heartache, and fallout after coming out. In this case, coming out is viewed an action. Done to others. Fair enough. However, living authentically is embracing your "who".

Guilt is a sneaky asshole because it often takes up space just beneath the surface. It is the silent killer of peace and enjoys sneaking up on you when you least expect it. I was shocked when guilt about Yvette's death recently came up in therapy. What could I possible feel guilty about? I did everything I could, followed her wishes, and loved her like no one else had in her life. Still, I felt a weight that was tough to put my finger on. During a particularly rough EMDR therapy session, more on that later, I found myself dealing head on with my own guilt that she died on my watch. Despite my efforts, she died anyway. Overcoming this installment of guilt means learning to separate the love we shared from her pain. Not an easy one, but I am slowly letting go and replacing the heaviness with lightness and joyful memories of her and I.

Choose growth over guilt. Be proud and loud about what you want your life to look like. Read that sentence again. Remember you are more than what you have done or what has happened to you in your life. Let go and see what happens.

REGRET

Even the most optimistic are not immune to experiencing occasional or lingering regrets. As much as we try, some things are harder to get past than others. Wishing a different choice had been made is my definition of a regret. There is a laundry list to choose from in the regret department. Regret comes in all shapes and sizes. Whether large, medium, or small, how we process it will determine how we think about life, ourselves, and the world around us.

Hindsight is the catalyst for regret. Our state of mind plays a vital role in how we process the choices we have made. Over the past few years, I have been a student in the school of regret more than any other time in my life. It is especially prevalent when I am feeling run down, emotionally exhausted, and frustrated.

One little drop can cascade into a waterfall if I allow my brain to get away from me. I am guilty of allowing regret to suck the wind out of my sails on more than one occasion. It is not pretty and feels terrible. We all have moments where we are just too tired to fight the wave of disappointment and focus on thoughts of what could have been…if only. What if I realized I was a lesbian earlier in life? What if I decided to ask for everything I was entitled to after I got divorced from my husband? What if I would have made Yvette go to the emergency room months earlier when she looked exhausted all the time? Insert your own regret here.

I watched a video asking strangers to write their biggest regret on a blackboard placed in the middle of a city street. The one common word that appeared most often was the word not. Three letters. Not going to college, not following their dreams, not spending more time with family were a few. After the video ended, I realized not only how crippling regrets can be, but also the enormous toll carrying the weight of regret has on our well-being.

Some regret things done, but most regret what was not done. My final decision to come out was fueled by my fear of getting to the end of my days and realizing I did not live an authentic life. Dealing with the mess that ensued was less terrifying than imagining myself closeted for the rest of my life.

There are times when we regret the things we said or actions we took which hurt other people. However, regret is often linked to the times we let ourselves down. Sure, there are some choices and regrets that cannot be redone or revisited to fix. You cannot undo getting married or having children for example.

Unless someone invents a time machine that offers a way to go back and change the past, we all face the challenge of learning to move beyond our regrets. Knowing some words, actions, or deeds cannot be undone may not offer much in the way of comfort, but it is comforting to know we can do differently in the future. You live and learn. Make the best of what is in front of you and focus on the positive.

Life is a journey which is full of endless opportunities, possibilities, and prospects. What is going on in between our ears greatly influences the decisions we make at any point in time. Regrets are present reminders of the times we failed, gave in to fear, or just plain dropped the ball for any number of reasons we thought were good at the time.

Finding a way to let go of and move beyond our past decisions, or indecision, is the only way to dump the excess baggage from our mental and emotional cargo hold. Dwelling on the things we cannot change strips away our ability to make peace with what was and prevents us from being able to focus on what is and what can be. We always have a choice. Regretting not taking a chance on something should not deter us from taking chances in the future.

Being stuck in the past steals joy and robs many of their peace. We are not bound by our past. If we do not remain committed to staying rooted in the present moment, the growing pile of garbage threatens to bury us. Emptying our brains of past emotional trash goes a long way in preventing the overflow and guarding against future regret.

Understanding the Past

Regardless of our situation, we are all capable of anything we set our minds to, work hard for, and deeply wish to accomplish. Regrets, if properly processed, teach us about ourselves more than anything else. We grow when we push past what our inner voices tell us and reach outside of our comfort zones.

Look at it this way, energy that is spent dwelling on regret is energy taken away from what is possible right now. Ask yourself where you would rather spend your energy. I encourage you to do something today that you have always wanted to do but never have. Start small and work your way up from there. Your mind, body, and spirit will thank you for it.

7 - NEGATIVITY

In 2016, as New Year's approached, the prevailing sentiment on social media focused on the need for the past year "to just be over." For sure the year personally challenged our family in ways we never expected, but was it really the worst year ever? Or did it just feel that way? What are the parameters for this bold statement? It is hard to forget the trying or unpleasant moments in a year. Cancer sucks. However, do these moments override all the good things which happened as well?

Yvette and I attended a "2016 Can Kiss My Ass" New Year's Eve party at our home away from home, The Venue, in Orlando. It seemed appropriate given the way the year ended. The truth is, it could have been called anything and we still would have been there. We were guilty of celebrating the end of a trying year with the "can't wait for it to be over" mentality. Our intention was for less cancer and more peace. Remaining positive in the face of a serious illness is not easy. Cancer changed the fabric of our lives, but the quilt was not completely trashed.

Negativity

As the clock struck midnight, we stood in the theater burst into tears. The relief of a crappy year passing and the uncertainty of what the new year would bring dripped down our cheeks. We were surrounded by friends, who are family, and the moment passed quickly. Chin up. Better days coming. Please.

Focusing on negative events like loss, sickness, or general blah is oppressive, suffocating, and extinguishes optimism and hope. It is like trying to walk barefoot through a room filled with broken lightbulbs without a flashlight.

If you see yourself in this scenario, fear not. There is a way out of this room. Each of us has an escape room challenge which is open year-round within the confines of our minds. No Groupon necessary. The clues to get out are there. Successfully locating them depends on our chosen mindset.

Developing an aversion to negativity takes time. Often, we classify negativity incorrectly. If someone is accustomed to negativity as the norm, it is tricky to see it for what it is. In healthy environments, pessimism and negativity are absent. Being consciously aware of inner thoughts and attitudes is difficult when internal negativity is calling the shots.

How we move through our moments, all of them, determines the quality and meaning of our journey. The way out of the room hinges on our choices. Some moments are heavy and making a choice to concentrate on the positive is easier said than done. Experience teaches that dwelling on the negative only delays and blocks the view of good things.

Curiously, a common source of internally created negativity is often around intimacy. More specifically, how we think others will react or think about us in the physical sense. Men and women alike struggle with fears about how they look or have the tendency to question their attractiveness. Insecurity thrives on negativity.

Women who have been through a divorce later in life, regardless of the reason, understand that aging, childbirth, and genetics are not our friends. As much as we would all jump at the chance to step back into our younger and more firm-bodied selves, it is just not possible. Damn.

Despite the toll age can have on our physical selves, there is hope. No, it is not at the hands of the best plastic surgeon in the country or the scientist who has yet to invent a time machine. Sorry. It is true. I researched it. So, what do we do in the absence of these two options?

In the spirit of full disclosure and transparency, I too have moments of struggling with how my body looks. None of us are immune to the bitchy little voice that always seems to pipe in after a big meal or when stepping out of the shower. Change magnifies our fear and can do a number on our self-esteem.

When Yvette and I were in the beginning stages of our new relationship, we were nervous about being intimate. Our chosen approach was to caution each other about every self-perceived flaw and shortcoming. It was dumb and did nothing to help take away the nerves. Truthfully, I did not care about whatever monsters lay

Negativity

beneath her clothes but still felt the need to warn her of my own. Can you relate? It was so unnecessary, but we did it.

In fact, when I finally saw her topless, I laughed. From what she described, I had been expecting an alien freak show and not the beautiful body that I saw in front of my eyes. A perfect reminder about how ridiculous our brains can be.

Allowing ourselves to be ruled by negativity and self-doubt is not conducive to creating a life of peace and confidence. This is where the work begins. Accepting ourselves includes how we look. We cannot profess to be confident and then want to hide and change what we look like because we do not think someone else is going to accept us.

Telegraphing insecurity is not the answer nor is warning the world of every stretch mark, fat roll, or squishy area. Our bodies are merely our earth suits. Who we are has nothing to do with how we look. Being comfortable with whatever you look like is the goal. If you look around, there are few, if any, that fit the model of perfection so many of us try to achieve. Worry clogs the engine running within our earth suits and eventually spills out into the world.

What if we decided to not verbalize and warn people of our flaws ahead of time? What would happen if we stopped painting ourselves in such a negative light? What would it feel like to let go of the fear we have about not being thin, pretty, or attractive enough for someone else to love? What would it feel like to tell the bitchy voice to shut up?

The way we see ourselves is what we project out in the world. I know I sound like a broken record, but it is true. Garbage in, garbage out. For those who are in the space between relationships and struggling with the intimacy gremlin, there is good news. We are much more critical of ourselves than any other could ever be.

Combatting negativity means saying thank you to someone who compliments you instead of pointing out something negative as a response. Whether you choose a quiet mantra or spray paint the affirmations on the walls of your living room is irrelevant. Just start somewhere. Changing our perspective goes a long way to propel us forward. Mindset is everything. Small changes will make way for huge gains in peace and pushing negativity away.

Releasing negativity is the ultimate weapon against fear and will clear the way for inner peace to grow. Cognitively speaking, the process of dealing with negativity is complex. There are some situations and circumstances which happen that simply cannot be overcome just by changing your internal dialogue. Enter trauma.

8 - DEALING WITH TRAUMA

When you hear the word trauma, what do you think of? Trauma tends to be viewed as major events which cause stress and discomfort. While this is true, trauma is not always caused by earth shattering events. Trauma is the result of brain wiring becoming tangled and losing the ability to function normally. When working properly, our brain processes information in a predictable way.

The events in our lives which we have no control over are as certain as the sun setting at night and rising in the morning. The Center for Treatment of Anxiety and Mood Disorders defines trauma as *"a psychological, emotional response to an event or an experience that is deeply distressing or disturbing. When loosely applied, this trauma definition can refer to something upsetting, such as being involved in an accident, having an illness or injury, losing a loved one, or going through a divorce. However, it can also encompass the far extreme and include*

experiences that are severely damaging, such as rape or torture."
1https://centerforanxietydisorders.com/what-is-trauma/

This definition provides a framework for unwrapping the complex impact trauma can have on our lives. The effects of trauma influence both the conscious and subconscious mind.

John Manuel-Andriote wrote, *"The meaning we attach to our experiences—how we explain them to ourselves—can have a huge impact on our psychological well-being. It can be the difference between shutting ourselves down with denial and shame, versus developing a sense of our own resilience that we can call upon the next time (there will always be a 'next time') we encounter adversity or suffer trauma (I call this "conscious resilience," as it involves consciously reminding ourselves of what we already have "lived to tell about.").*"[1]

Life events or stimuli can interrupt the normal processing system causing it to misfire. Understanding how the brain processes information seems like a good place to begin. Zachary Gleason, MSW, LCSW, and owner of Bronze Star Counseling, gave me a crash course on the mechanics of trauma. On a good day, our brains are designed to process information in a predictable circuit. Each part of the circuit does its job when working properly.

When something happens, the brain stem is the first stop on the train. The brain stem is responsible for the autonomic nervous system activities and handling unconscious bodily functions such as breathing, heart rate, and digestion. Information then travels through the limbic system, which is the emotion center of the brain.

Dealing with Trauma

The amygdala acts like the traffic cop looking for danger and flags potentially dangerous information.

The information then passes through the front right hemisphere which is where raw emotion, sensation, and visualization resides. The front left hemisphere is the next stop on the circuit. This area is where language, logic, and reason reside. If all goes well, the event then makes it way to the central portion of the brain where everything is categorized, and a fully formed memory can be stored. Boom. All is good in the brain.

Sometimes though, the amygdala freaks out. The flight or fight response lives here. When this happens, the body shuts down all non-essential functions and metabolic processes are paused. In this case, the left front hemisphere shuts down too. This is where the problem happens. It is like putting a spoke in a moving bicycle tire. The ability to use language, logic, or reason disappears. A bottleneck happens when the circuit breaks. The feeling right side is now running the show.

Raw terror is the amygdala's reaction to a perceived danger. When it is running the show, adrenalin is released and the left hemisphere's ability to explain and label what is happening disappears. This is the fight or flight response in action. The result is terror which has nowhere to go. It just floats around the right brain. When the perceived dangerous situation ends, the natural process of the body dealing with the aftermath kicks in. When all systems come back online, the left brain should pull the information from the log jam and process it. If this happens, you are good to go. Just another memory stored for future use.

The problem happens when the right brain holds these feelings hostage. The brain is always trying to repair and protect itself from damage. Unprocessed emotions cause the brain to create a hard shell around these damaged axons. The brain is trying to compartmentalize and erect a roadblock for the damaged tissue. When the whole brain tries to process the event, the hard shell prevents processing from happening, resulting in post-traumatic stress. PTSD is a memory processing disorder and not a mental disorder.

Stuck memories in the right side of the brain cannot be processed by the left brain, which means the memory cannot be stored. Nightmares are frequently the first manifestation of PTSD. Dreaming is a natural process where the brain decides what material to toss and which to store. The body uses REM sleep to process our thoughts and experiences.

Understanding trauma's ability to alter the brain is a science lesson. How do we move past trauma once the damage is done? Moving past trauma is not automatic. If peace and healing is the goal, learning how to move through the events which created unprocessed memories is step one.

The impact of unprocessed trauma on the body is still being discovered. When the body is in a constant, often subconscious, state of fight or flight, it becomes less able to function normally. Carrying unprocessed crap can cause autoimmune disease, hypertension, and diabetes. The body is programmed to adjust and rebalance when things go off the rails. The brain secretes chemicals and hormones to remedy the imbalance. Living in a constant state of unprocessed memories takes a toll on the body and changes us on a cellular level.

The process to rewire the brain and change how we react to triggers is hard work and may require professional help. Ugh. I know. The dreaded "T" word is going to be thrown around here. Therapy is successful if you are willing to do the work religiously and venture to the dark and scary places. Many think just acknowledging the trauma is the key to letting go and healing. If only it was that easy.

Understanding and naming the trauma sounds like step one, however the nature of trauma shows us that naming is not possible for stuck right brain memories. For those who have buried events which occur in any stage of life this can be a terrifying option. Why would anyone want to reopen long past wounds? My late wife was convinced she was going to find some secret method or shortcut to dealing with the numerous traumas she faced in her lifetime.

She was resistant and fought dealing with the emotional, mental, spiritual, and physical effects of being mentally and physically abused as a child, and emotionally abused in her 22-year marriage. Despite my best efforts to convince her to seek help, she side stepped the process for years. She did go to therapy a few times, but her triggers never were discussed. She kept it light and airy. She was not ready to do the work.

The fear of being overcome by the emotions was greater than the desire to change her reactions. She was stubborn that way. Only after we were married did she agree to finally, and honestly, address the underlying trauma which was fueling the problems cropping up in our relationship. Her self-image was skewed and the filter she viewed life through was making her miserable. Her determination to move past the past was not enough to propel her on a healing trajectory.

Her approach was an intellectual one. Instead of dealing with the emotions she focused on trying to understand why things happened like they did and drove herself crazy in the process. Dealing with trauma is not like fixing a flat tire or changing out old spark plugs. In order to truly get past the things that were causing her anxiety and abandonment issues, she needed to emotionally process the impact.

Knowing her mother suffered from insecurity and shame regarding her own past did little to stem the tide for herself. Nor did it make learning at the age of thirteen, in a rage filled moment, that the man she believed to be her father was not her birth father any easier. Her mother's shame surrounding how my late wife came into the world colored every minute of her childhood and helped to create not only low self-esteem but also a dangerous eating disorder.

In therapy she learned the eating disorder was an attempt to gain some sense of control over something in her life. Knowing why did not help lessen her obsession with how she looked or what she weighed. It did not stop her from marrying a controlling man or believing that just because he never hit her that she was not being abused. When we became a couple, she was not sure how to handle the lack of chaos in her new life.

She believed that starting over as her authentic self would automatically heal the wounds of the past. Shelving the past was her specialty. Being with me, in a new environment, was a blessing. She finally had a safe, healthy place with the freedom and support which was lacking in her life up to that point. My understanding and patience got tested many times while she attempted to work through the demons from her past.

Therapy allowed her to address major issues for the first time, however new ones surfaced. When she came out, her son took it hardest and his struggles affected our entire family. He made it clear that he wanted nothing to do with her. The reaction of her son was completely unexpected and was devastating. Years were spent trying to accommodate him, yet he continued to treat her poorly. She felt responsible for how he was behaving because, after all, she raised him.

She truly believed she had done something wrong and bent over backwards to remedy her self-perceived parental failings. She parented him differently than she was parented, yet never felt like she was doing a good enough job raising him. The not good enough dialogue was deeply engrained, and she held herself to the fire with a vengeance. The trauma of her childhood was the filter through which she saw herself.

When he was with us, it felt like the walls of our house wouldn't be able to withstand the chaos. Her ex did everything in his power to make her life miserable which compounded the situation and made for hellish visits.

We were sensitive to her son's needs and twisted ourselves into pretzels trying to ease his discomfort. Despite our efforts to accommodate his feelings, he was never appeased, and we felt like he was acting as an agent for his father. We were walking on eggshells and nothing we did to help him adjust was making a difference. He did not want to be a part of our family and made it known at every turn. We wanted so desperately for things to be different, but no progress was made in achieving that goal.

The little time he spent with us resulted in the same unrest she had been living with before she moved out. We weren't optimistic about anything changing given the negativity he was exposed to when he was at his dad's house. He was supposed to live with us and go to school in our town. This proved to be too much for him to handle. He too struggled with anxiety and leaving the home he had grown up in was something which would have added to his mental and emotional struggle.

Losing the relationship with her son was traumatic for Yvette. Rightfully so. Her left brain and right brain were at war her entire life. Intellectually processing a traumatic event is only the beginning. Acknowledging the abuse or trauma can take years and is emotionally draining. Once this step is reached, you can move through the door and begin to heal.

She realized that no matter what she did, it would never be enough to create a healthy relationship with him. Only intense EMDR therapy brought her to the point where she could finally let him know how he treated her was not acceptable and let herself off the hook for his choices and behavior. Without this therapy, the healing

Dealing with Trauma

process was not possible. So, what is EMDR and how can it help with trauma?

EMDR stands for Eye Movement Desensitization and Reprocessing. Francine Shapiro's work in the area of EMDR therapy is based on the Adaptive Information Processing Model. Her book *"Getting Past Your Past; Take Control of Your Life with Self-Help Techniques from EMDR Therapy"* is a great resource for anyone interested in learning about this form of therapy. In layman's terms, EMDR is an effective tool for forcing the brain to reprocess the unprocessed emotions and memories which got stuck in the right brain.

Imagine your brain is like a car engine. When at a stop light, the engine is running around 750 rpms. If you press on the gas while the car is in park the rpms increase but the car stays put. EMDR artificially raises the activity level in the center part of the brain. Revving the engine not only speeds up the engine but it creates more power. By thinking of the memories which are stuck and hitting the gas, the left brain can pull the information over and process it. Remember, the left side is where logic, reason, and language reside. This allows the brain to make sense of the terror and shines a light on the memories and releasing the pain. It can be filed in the "just another experience" folder in the central part of the brain.

Therapists who are trained in this technique use lights, hands, or a variety of techniques which bilaterally stimulate the brain to get the engine revving. Her therapist used lights. By watching a light move back and forth on a platform while bringing forward painful memories, she was able to process and release the grip of the past trauma.

For children and adults, the processing time is different. Children have less experience and frame of reference due to their young age. As a result, processing usually does not take as long as someone who has more life experience. A seventy-year-old adult might have a seventy-story building compared to a twenty-year old's twenty stories of memories and experiences. Given this, processing does not happen instantaneously. On the days Yvette had EMDR therapy, she was spent and was advised to avoid anything mentally taxing, even work. There were days she was quiet and days when she cried for hours afterward.

Allowing emotions to be processed is a temporary drag, but living a life filled with fear, nightmares, anxiety, and depression is no picnic either. As adults, we owe ourselves the gift of wellness. Mentally, emotionally, and physically speaking. Taking care of ourselves begins with a firm commitment to handle our shit, even if it involves asking for outside help. Resources are everywhere. Operating under the "screwed up adults raise screwed up children" theory, addressing trauma is a critical step in preventing a pattern from becoming a way of being. Handling our own shit is the only way to safeguard the next generation from further harm.

The example we set for our children is only as good as we are. Again, trauma, if unchecked, creates long term effects on health and wellness. Authenticity requires an honest look at our mindset and the list of items we toss up on the shelf hoping it will go away if we ignore it. It does not. Anxiety is a hallmark of trauma. Dialing in to our children and understanding their experience of the world during their formative years will color how they see the world, and the quality of their lives is so important.

As adults, we are responsible for our own choices and wellness. The cause of anxiety in children can be as simple as a parent coming home late from work one night. One moment of fear can create a lifetime of worry and irrational thinking about the safety and well-being of anyone in their lives. Tuning in to a child's mindset and stepping in when they exhibit signs of anxiety will be key in their evolution into happy, healthy, and functioning adults.

LETTING GO

When life is exploding, the act, or mere mention of the idea of letting go is impossible when hanging on requires a strong grip. The hurricane must pass before the damage assessment and clean up can proceed.

Thoughts, feelings, and emotions produce debris in our lives which must be cleaned up before we can entertain the idea of letting go. Letting go is not possible until the debris is picked up, sorted, and properly disposed of.

The timeline for clean-up varies. There is no schedule. Fortunately, radar may be able to predict the pace and direction of the storm but dealing with the aftermath is not so cut and dry. For some events, letting go happens organically and without much thought. Time can bring healing, but if you are fifty stories above the ground dangling in mid-air, time may not be of much help. A death grip is exhausting.

Moving Through

Often, dwelling on the emotion of where we were causes us to fail to consider the progress we have made. Self-doubt and regret are stubborn companions that kicking the brain into overdrive at a moment's notice. Making peace with the past includes letting go of the need to rethink and analyze events that are no longer relevant to the present moment.

There is beauty in the past we often gloss over or forget, especially when we relive negative moments repeatedly. Memories can be a double-edged sword when a thinker decides to stroll down memory lane. There is a time and place for careful consideration and thinking, however a cautious brain in a constant thought spasm creates more problems than solutions, or peace.

Letting go of the past and getting over the past are two different things. How do you tell someone to just get over the fact they were physically or sexually abused? What about someone who experienced a devastating loss, illness, or lived in a home that was consumed by the cycle of addiction?

Getting over it is not an option. Some things are impossible to just get over. Letting go is another story. While some things may be impossible to fully get over, the ability to move forward is always an option. Moving past, and through, can open the door to healing. Letting go does not mean forgetting what happened. Rather it is the decision to refuse to allow the effects of the past filter into the present. Learning how to let go is the most important aspect of finding peace. For those who experienced traumatic events in their past, this is a tough sell.

Dealing with Trauma

The process of moving forward begins with a long, hard look back. While painful, it is the first step of the stairwell of peace. In order to let go, you must acknowledge the existence, impact, and effects of whatever has happened in life.

Processing personal baggage is not an option, but rather a necessity. In the days after being released from the hospital, Yvette asked me if I had planned to write any blogs. At first, I chalked her constant questioning up to the good drugs, as she was not very lucid. I soon realized she was serious. My response was the same each time. No. Who wanted to read about drains, tumors, death, and loss? That was all I had. My baggage was overpacked.

My reasons were plenty. First, I did not feel like it. Second, I had nothing to say. My message of peace and fearlessness was going to be a stretch. I was neither. Even filled with pain medication, my wife was pushing me forward. I had a decision to make. In the weeks before her double mastectomy, I seriously considered ending my blog and *Switching Teams* book journey. Obviously, I did not. I was feeling overwhelmed and lacked any control over what was happening around me. So, in true Dawn form, I reacted by thinking about something I had some control over. My book. I am nothing if not predictable.

What do you do when the present moment includes gifts that have smashed bows and brown paper held together with dental floss? Be fearless and authentic anyway. Yuk. I reached this conclusion as I dropped off the bag of my wife's bras at the donation site. I drove up and did not get out of the car. I rolled down the window, grabbed the fancy hospital personal belongings bag from the passenger seat, handed them to the attendant, and declined a receipt. Simple enough, right?

Nope. Before the window was up, I lost it. The timing was shocking and unexpected. I had ten other places to go and was completely caught off guard by the emotional flood gates swinging open. Reality hit. Despite an abundance of difficult moments, none snuck up on me like this one. Waiting during surgery, talking to the surgeon afterward, or emptying drains did not register as reality. Yvette needed me to be strong and put together. I had a job to do and my emotions were neatly stuffed away.

Fair warning. Reality is sometimes raw and unavoidable. There were many moments in the months after Yvette died when I struggled to find the bright and shiny side. In December 2016, within a twenty-four-hour period, my stepmom died, and my wife underwent a double mastectomy. The grieving process for my stepmom was put on hold. Every bit of my energy needed to be focused on taking care of my wife as she recovered from her surgery and began adjusting to her new flat and fabulous life.

My thoughts were scattered and often about my dad and how he was doing. My dad and I are cut from the same cloth. My wife joked about how similar we are in our approach to life and handling things. I believe the word she preferred to use was clone. We would rather do something than discuss feelings. Our shared dislike of being emotionally uncomfortable and not being able to fix things for those we love is legendary.

Dealing with Trauma

The timing of everything was a curve ball neither of us could hit. He had a head start in the "my wife has cancer" race. We both share a common dislike for sickness and hospitals. For two years, I watched my dad take incredible care of the love of his life. He was a rock for Diana. Watching him was inspiring and helped remind me of my own strength and courage.

As Yvette was preparing for surgery, my dad was sitting in hospice. I was not able to reach out to him for one of his epic pep talks because of the circumstances. His struggle became my strength. If he could do this, I could too. We all could. This was his and Diana's early gift to me. The holidays were different that year.

The lessons of that dark season were that I could handle much more than I thought I could. I learned that the sum of the Waters Chicks was assuredly greater than our separate parts. My late wife was a warrior and the most inspiring person I knew. Our hope was found in the little victories. I relished the joy which came from taking a break to watch my son play goalie for the high school varsity soccer team or sitting on the couch with my family. Those moments were reminders that it was possible to feel peace in the storm.

Dealing with traumatic events is a part of life. Being thrown for a loop, often without warning, is how life not so gently reminds us of how little control we have over what happens. Even so, the journey can be beautiful even if it is not always pretty or wrapped in expensive silver paper and adorned with perfect bows.

9 - GRIEF

I not only lost a spouse, but my best friend. Our ten-year best friendship preceded our partnering and formed the foundation for our relationship. Losing both at the same time was the worst. When bad things happen, we reach out to our besties for comfort, wisdom, and strength. My bestie was truly the best. Despite her absence, I have survived. The wounds are slowly healing, and breathing is a little easier each day, but she is missed terribly by us all.

She died on November 26, 2017 and I chose December 17th for her memorial service. I told everyone I wanted to allow the boys to finish their semesters at school. They had enough on their plates. I lied. I was broken and needed three weeks to prepare for this "celebration" of life. Her final wishes were for a party where people could dance.. Also known as "A death party." Her words, not mine. Great. I agreed but regretted it immediately after she died.

I was too busy not eating and getting through the minutes to plan a grand event, so I asked for help. Oh, wait. Delegated? Does that sound better? That is the same as asking for help, right? In any case, I passed the buck. I was too sad to get dressed let alone coordinate a funeral. The day after she died, I went to the cremation office. My 18-year-old son drew the short straw and accompanied me. We sat down and the kind woman working asked if he was my brother. It is the little things. We glanced at the wall of urns and knew she would have hated them all.

The urn search on Amazon yielded more of the same. I briefly entertained the idea of building something for her cremains. Ridiculous. I was barely functioning and a wood working project was not going to happen. Instead, we bought a small pelican box. Photographers use these boxes to store or transport cameras and I knew she would appreciate the fact that it only cost $35. Win, win.

Aside from the death of grandparents, my experience of grief was limited in my lifetime. I was shielded from the discomfort as a child. The losses in my adult life were thankfully limited. Losing my marriage after coming out was my first soul shattering experience of deep grief. No one died, but loss is loss. My first up close and personal experience of the dying process happened in 2014 when Yvette's mother died.

My logical brain was not wired to weather the emotional magnitude of grief. Forty-six years of living did not prepare me for what losing my wife would feel like. There was no way to put my head down and power through it. There were no mind tricks to help lessen the pain. My authentic self was a puddle on the floor. Each night as the sun went down, I experienced panic attacks. The night was not my friend for a very long time.

Moving Through

Doing one small thing every day to move through the pain was exhausting. Every time I turned around there was a new task I would have to face alone. Showering was often the most I accomplished in a day. On a good day, I ventured out but only for a short period of time. This cliff was unchartered territory. My usual tether and safety latch were gone. Seven days of watching Yvette courageously fight the sneaky monster inside of her forever changed me. Which is the fancy way of saying it broke me. For the first time in my life I felt truly alone. My core shifted and I was flat out leveled.

She and I had operated as a unit for many years. In our seven years as a couple, we were apart two nights. Once for her hysterectomy in 2014, and then again the night she had the double mastectomy. I would have stayed in the room with her, but she insisted I go home and sleep in a real bed. She would not take no for an answer. Happy wife, happy life.

Grief was my new uninvited best friend and companion that finally evicted the cancer squatter. Training for the grief marathon was pointless. It showed up at the door with a loud whistle, broken stopwatch, and a box of tissues. My grief marathon officially began on a Saturday night and is still a part of my daily workout. Experiencing the death of my best friend and wife rearranged my DNA and changed me in ways I am still discovering. Moving through this loss is now part of my forever journey.

I retreated inside of myself when possible but did not shut down completely. My loneliness was interrupted only when I could imagine her yelling at me to wash my face and brush my nasty

Grief

teeth. I kept going because she could not. It was an impossible task, but minute by minute I kept going. It was not pretty or graceful. I did not care. The feeling was like nothing else. It was sadness, but so much more. My bones ached.

Sadness and grief are not the same thing. Sadness is one of many regular everyday feelings. A friend cancelling dinner plans or hearing bad news can cause sadness. Grief is sadness, anger, and shock jacked up to a new level. Grief is no joke.

How are you doing? An innocent and caring enough question but one I had a tough time answering. From a young age, my boys hated being sick. To help them cope when they were down for the count with an illness, I reminded them each passing minute was one minute closer to them feeling well again. Things will get better. Be patient. Look on the bright side. This too shall pass.

Knowing an ending point was on the horizon helped them get through the discomfort and unpleasant symptoms. Fortunately, strep throat, stomach bugs, or sinus infections go away. What happens when the "shall pass" is a loved one?

Each day, I clung to the hope that every passing minute might bring me one day closer to not feeling the loss of my wife so deeply. I missed her in my soul. Each morning, my first thoughts were focused on whether this would be the day life would return to some semblance of normal. Well, new normal anyway, whatever that means. My optimistic side hoped so, but new normal is a long-term commitment and on most days is a decent kick in the ass. Grief is not for the impatient.

Moving Through

NEW NORMAL

Life without my wife looked a lot like it did when she was still alive, however felt nothing like it. Figuring out what to do with the emotions was like bringing home a new baby. In this case, a newborn with colic and reflux. I am both parent and child in the new normal. I can identify with the parental struggle to soothe, comfort, and offer relief while simultaneously feeling the discomfort of the colicky baby.

Additionally, I was on grief's schedule, not the other way around. It is impossible to predict or prepare for the random breakdowns, waves of tears, or onset of zombie brain fog. It was a guessing game and especially unsettling when the waves hit in public. My first few ventures out were ugly and teary. Yes, I was the one crying while waiting at the deli counter or picking out cereal when Drops of Jupiter by Train played on the speakers in the store. I learned to block out the background music at the grocery store while I shopped to avoid those uncomfortable stares from strangers who had no idea what my problem was.

I was now a member of the exclusive deceased spouse's club. I am both devastated and honored to be among the rank and file. Without giving away too many details about the group rules, the best part of the meetings is exchanging "stupid shit people say after losing a spouse" stories. Surprisingly enough, sarcasm and humor does heal. The day I cleared out her dresser I found a stash of money. The next moment, I watched a palmetto bug climb out of her underwear drawer and laughed. I told the kids it was a good thing she was dead already because she would have died if she saw that. After the house was set on fire, of course.

The best piece of advice I received from those walking a similar path was to give myself permission to feel everything and take time to sit in the emotions. Ugh. As much as I would like to say my decision to feel was intentional, I did so because I had no choice. Sometimes putting one foot in front of the other looks more like sitting in a mud puddle for a minute or two.

GRIEF REALITY CHECK

Though determined to move through the grieving process fully and without skipping steps, I secretly hoped for the big red easy button to appear on my dresser each morning. No such luck. Here are some lessons grief taught me.

Grief Reality #1: Losing a loved one is difficult. There is no way to prepare other than to make sure you have a reliable band of foxhole buddies who are willing to sit in the dirt with you, often at a moment's notice. Choose those who do not scare easily. No, seriously, this is huge. It will get ugly and may involve vomiting or hyperventilation. This is a critical piece of the puzzle and will make all the difference as you navigate the grieving process.

Grief Reality #2: Toss any preconceived notions, ideas, or estimations about what grief looks like right out the window. Dealing with death, divorce, or any loss feels like playing dodgeball with boulders and bullets on a racquetball court. There are no rules, instructions, referees, or ticking clock involved.

Grief Reality #3: This one is important and my least favorite. Logic is powerless against grief. There are plenty of sources for advice, suggestions, and what to expect when a loved one dies. However, absorbing any information or wisdom is very difficult. Survival mode blocks any intellect. Reading books, talking about it, and creating a plan of action to cope with grief sounds great on paper, but realistically is just busy work. You cannot outthink grief. It is an asshole that way.

Grief Reality #4: Do the work. There is no way around this one and it is my co-least favorite. It is often ugly, messy, and what utterly broken looks like. Do it anyway. Do it for you and your lost loved one. Do it for your family and friends. Doing the work means briefly surrendering to every irrational thought, regret, instant replay, sleepless night, and would, could, should have scenario and then moving through it. Repeatedly. The work heals. Every day. Over and over. Do the work.

(Helpful hint: Puffy eyes, dark circles, and headaches will let you know if you are doing it correctly.)

Grief Reality #5: The journey is not a straight shot to the destination. Googling traffic conditions is pointless on this route. The landscape and weather changes without warning. The destination is not on any map, but arrival is guaranteed only by putting one foot in front of the other each day. Some moments in the journey will take longer to get through. Frequent rest stops are recommended.

Grief

The grief journey is not a one size fits all proposition. The greatest lesson grief teaches is life is short, precious, and beautiful. The new normal is different, but surprisingly good. I have laughed, cried, felt numb, screamed, yelled, and even punched a wall in a brief fit of anger. Not my finest moment, but I own it. Every emotion has been necessary and has brought healing to areas I did not realize needed to be addressed.

If only the profound grief we experienced could be lightened by a glimpse of the finish line. None of us are distance runners but the long haul is building our distance skills. Looking for the silver lining in these clouds is challenging when the storm is raging outside. There are lessons in everything. I still cannot comprehend the reason why my wife, best friend, and person died from metastatic breast cancer within a week of it being found in her whole body.

TIMELINES

The concept of timelines took on a new meaning after her death. Counting the days was one way to remind myself to keep moving forward. Marking time helps us get a gauge of where we have been, are, or will be headed. The school year is a perfect example. Those with children know what I am talking about and understand the ebb and flow of life when school is in and out of session.

The school calendar is predictable and set. How we handle our days may not be so clear cut. Life is about choices. Despite our best efforts to control what our day looks like, sometimes it just does not work out how we thought or hoped for.

As I drove home in a mental fog from hospice, I decided I was going to give myself six months to figure out how to maneuver through life without my best friend and wife. It is the only thought I remember from that surreal ride back to my house; which hours earlier had been our house.

In that moment, I gave myself permission to let go of any expectations and time to figure out what the hell just happened. Processing something so sudden and devastating is not a short-term job. Without getting too morose, everything changed at 2 am on November 26th, 2017. My kids and I had a new moment which became a significant marker in time.

Focusing on a timeline offered perspective and was a source of comfort and, as usual, lessons. The first lesson was debunking the myth that timelines are inflexible. They are mere suggestions and a mental guide for moving forward toward a goal. A countdown to a vacation one is of few timelines that is typically not going to change. On this day, we leave. Pretty straight forward. If only the rest were so set in stone. Adhering to a timeline is a great goal but be prepared for the unexpected obstacles waiting to trip you up.

The second lesson is that there is no timeline for when a timeline should end. I searched high and low for it. It does not exist though many think it does. There are often unspoken expectations for how someone who loses a spouse should behave or live. I know. I had them too. Until I joined the widows club.

There is no timeline for grief, moving on with a new person, or just getting back to some semblance of normal. To each their own in its purest form. What works for one, does not work for all. Understanding this is a tough concept to grasp if you have not experienced significant loss. We can't always walk miles in other people's shoes especially when they are funeral shoes.

Each day was a mix of letting go, hanging on, and being grateful for the present moment. Again, dealing with grief is a marathon, not a sprint. Damn.

As the days continued to pass, embracing each as a brand-new opportunity for healing helped create space for a new relationship, outlook, and growth. Moving through the pain and experiencing new joy, love, and hope for the future helped me adjust to living in a space where the capacity for both extremes existed.

Remembering and honoring the promises made forced me to continue to practice what I preached about being fearless and nonjudgmental towards others and their choices. Thanks learning curve. Dangling timelines and preconceived ideas about how things are supposed to be were never my favorite things.

My self-imposed six-month timeline came and went. I thought it would be enough time to grieve and become accustomed to my new reality. In some ways, time healed. In others, it did not. Grief 101 says this is typical after experiencing a loss. Reaching the halfway point in the "year of firsts" was an accomplishment which was impossible to envision on November 27, 2017. Knowing forward momentum was only a moment away from a surprise brake check was unsettling, but not the worst thing in the world.

Simply put, without challenges growth is slow. Whatever challenges you may be facing in your life, remember to embrace every emotion and not fight the process. Or punch things. Learning how to be grateful for the dark is the key to peace. Without the darkness, you will not be able to fully appreciate the light.

Yvette was the soft place where we landed when times were tough. In her absence, the four of us became one another's safe place. She taught us well without even realizing it. One week my youngest came home from an outing and told me he gave a dollar to a homeless man outside of a doughnut shop. He said, "that's what she would have done."

Every tear we shed, word of encouragement shared, and photo is a reminder of how lucky we were to have her in our lives. In the meantime, in between the waves of grief, we focused on keeping her memory alive and behaving in ways which would make her proud. This is how we began moving through. Although she is not here physically, we feel her and know if she could be here in the frat house with us, she would.

NO SHORTCUTS

The idea that the only way out of something is through has been reinforced and proven thousands of times over. As much as I hoped to discover a shortcut to the grieving process, I am glad I didn't. Any plans to blow through the yellow light were tossed a long time ago.

There are no universal rules or approach to grief. I have grown infinitely since my wife died and feel more gratitude than I ever

Grief

imagined possible. It sounds crazy to associate grief and loss with gratitude, yet here I am doing it. Here is how that happened. We kept a safe in our closet for valuables. She was a pro at opening the safe. It was old school with a turn dial.

My attempts always ended with calling for her to come get the damn thing opened. Soon after her death, I needed to open the safe to grab her life insurance policy. I hoped the safe would miraculously open on the first try. It did not happen. By the twelfth attempt I was sweating, in tears, and pounding on the top of it. I took one deep breath and stared at the instructions one last time before looking up how to purchase dynamite online. I made one last plea for some other worldly help for a successful safe opening. Slowly to the left, slowly to the right, back to the left and boom. It opened.

I emptied the contents and gifted it to a neighbor the next day. Reminders of her were everywhere after she died. I grabbed a pen from the pen drawer to fill out and sign the life insurance papers. Of course, the pen was from the cancer center, which she pocketed after the last visit to the oncologist. The appointment which showed normal ranges for her blood work only two months prior to her death.

I learned more about myself, the world, and people since her death than any other time in my life. I continue to make peace with my emotions, rediscover myself, mend broken relationships which seemed irreparable, practice forgiveness, let go of resentments and regrets, embrace change, and I even opened myself up to the possibility of loving someone new.

10 - NEW DAWN. NEW DAY. NEW LIFE.

Sometimes moving through resembles moving on after someone important dies. The speed at which things change can be overwhelming and unexpected. The last thing on my mind was finding anyone new to share my life. Yvette always told me she would want me to find love again if something should happen to her. She also believed that I would be fine should the unthinkable transpire. She was wrong. Entertaining the idea of being with anyone but her was never on my radar.

Not for a moment. Ever. She knew me better than anyone. So much so, that the first words out of her mouth after the ER doc told us "it's not good" were to "let someone love me." I was having no part of the conversation. She was deadly serious, literally, and made me promise. I agreed just so we could end the conversation. The thought made me sick to my stomach, but I promised.

After two months of sitting Shiva, MJ, one of my foxhole buddies, thought I should begin expanding my circle and meet some new people. Ugh. Peopling was hard before losing my wife and the thought cramped my brain. Reluctantly, I let her set up a profile for me on a dating site. Letting someone else write a profile about you is interesting. Of course, I ended up editing it. My screen name was *befearless*.

"I have a great sense of humor, can be silly, but also enjoy connecting with people on a deeper level. Looking for someone who is willing to go slow and get to know each other first.

Hobbies include not judging books by the cover, all things sportsy, being authentic and fearless, and writing. My life is an open book, literally, but the unedited story is reserved for a small circle. My taste in music is eclectic and not for everyone's ears.

Finding someone who is comfortable in her own skin and values the importance of maintaining balance in all areas of life is a prerequisite and non-negotiable. Looking forward to seeing who is up for a challenge.

footnote: interests include being near the water, cooking, writing, watching sports, solving the mysteries of life, creating joy, and living fearlessly" befearless

I made it clear in my profile that I was looking for friends only. I decided to be blunt and honest about where I was and what had happened. Full disclosure is my jam. There would be no misunderstanding my delicate state nor any questions about my intentions.

My dating days were a distant memory. I was twenty when I met my husband, was with him for 20 years, then came out and began my late in life lesbian adventure with my best friend of ten years. If math is not your thing, I was almost thirty years out of the dating pool. Ugh.

Yet here I was dipping my toe in the friends-first dating pool. Honestly, the only reason I agreed was the promise I made. In addition to the lecture about letting someone love me, I also was sternly told to not stop living because she was going to die. Living was not sitting on the couch staring at the television or keeping a pillow in her spot on the bed so it would not look empty when I walked into the bedroom.

Working on Yvette's computer made me feel close to her. One random evening, I found myself sitting at her computer perusing the dating site. If nothing else, it was entertaining. Some women thought it fun to post profiles written from the perspective of their pet espousing the amazing qualities of their owner who was looking for love. I wish I was kidding.

Describing what happened next is difficult. My laughter was interrupted when I saw a profile for someone called DJ. I felt like I should look at this one. I cannot explain why. The feeling was like a tap on the shoulder. Honestly, the profile pic was not her best, so I flipped through the other photos she posted. One photo of her hugging her son as he left for navy boot camp spoke to me. Despite my interest, I did nothing. I walked away from the computer feeling oddly curious about her.

New Dawn. New Day. New Life

THE UNIVERSE

When my wife died, my friend Robin, who founded Libby's Legacy Breast Cancer Foundation, suggested I contact her friend who also lost her wife to breast cancer five years prior. This connection was invaluable as the days passed. Cathy and I spoke on the phone and she just got it. The pain, the gallows humor, the way life changes, and mechanics of grief and moving on. Our first conversation began with her saying "Well, I would ask how you are doing, but I know that is a dumb question so we will skip that."

One conversation included future relationships. Her wisdom was priceless. Her advice was to begin putting out to the universe what my wants and needs were for a new relationship. She did so after her spouse passed thinking it would take some time for the universe to work things out and balance the grief with some joy. Seven months later she met her partner.

I took this advice to heart and decided I would do the same. I temporarily set aside my anger at the universe and contemplated my must-have list. It was much shorter than I expected and included three things. Sitting on my closet floor, I lit a candle hoping it would not catch any of the clothes hanging on fire. Our closet was sacred. It was the place for us to have important conversations or just hide from the chaos of three boys and a dog. The spare pillows on the floor made an excellent lesbian lounge and adult fort.

After a few tears and some deep breaths, I made it known to the universe my request for someone who was comfortable in their own skin, confident, accepting and able to deal with the fact that my wife passed, and a mother. Being unspecific left some wiggle room for the universe to surprise me. I did not have the desire nor the energy to be picky about superficial things like appearance, political views, career choice, or socio-economic status. Greed was not something I thought the universe would respond kindly to or appreciate. Understanding, compassionate, confident, and kind seemed like a reasonable request.

What my late wife and I had was irreplaceable. Our relationship was unique and could never be replicated. Every relationship is different and has its own personality. Even in my darkest moments, I knew the impossibility of replacing Yvette and was realistic about any future relationships having their own personality and dynamic.

Cathy also prepared me for the reactions of people and what to expect when a new person entered the fold. Her wise words helped me to focus less on what people might think of me and to trust my instincts. The impact of her willingness to walk me through this shitty, uncharted territory and be my grief whisperer is something I will never be able to thank her enough for.

MY DAWN

Two weeks after my closet universe ritual, I received a wink. If you know what this is, you are smarter than I was. Upon further investigation, I noticed a comment under a photo of mine that said "nic pic." That is not a typo. I called MJ, also known as my online profile consultant, and asked her what to do. She sarcastically said

"Um. Say thank you." So, I did. It was from DJ. Two minutes later another message popped up.

"I am recently single too from being in a long-term relationship looking for some new people to hang out with." I did not respond until the next day. It was New Year's Eve and the second "first" holiday without my wife. The message was a welcome distraction from the pity party which was transpiring. At 11:41 p.m. I sent a response.

"Hey there. Thanks for the wink. Full disclosure...this is my first-time messaging or even being on a dating site. I am a newbie." Eleven minutes after 2018 began, she replied *"So am I. This is all new to me as well. Totally love your hairstyle. Looking forward to a new year in 2018......"*

Fifteen minutes later, I replied *"I am hoping to meet some new people but so far it is pretty scary...some of the pics I just cannot understand...but that's just me..."*

Her response was *"Exactly. What I am looking for is a new group of people. I joined a couple weeks back and looking for people with the same interests to do things with and if something sparks with someone, great."*

Clearly, she had a keen eye for great hair and seemed to be looking for the same thing. Friendship and meeting new people after experiencing an unexpected change in life. Okay universe, I'll bite.

We graduated to email soon after and realized we shared the same first name. She shared more details about her job and how she caught her wife having a relationship with a fellow teacher at her school in September. Both of us had seen better days for sure. We were both grieving losses and adjusting to life after the end of relationship.

I did not mention my wife passing until she brought up what happened with her marriage. She was in New York for the holiday visiting with her navy son who was deployed in Japan.

"It has been a tough few months for me as well. My 17-year relationship with my wife has ended. It was a complete shock to me. She hit 50 and midlife crisis hit. Maybe one day we can talk about things over coffee. It might be nice for a change to talk to an outsider. I am in NY freezing my butt off until 1/7. I have been off for the last two weeks. I have a great job that I have been at for 17 years. I am in sales and cover the entire state of Florida. Always need a break for coffee. We are both in sales and I bet our personalities are a lot alike. Have a great week. Dawn"

She was feeling awful about her situation until I told her about mine.

"I am very sorry to hear this. When you get back, and have thawed from the northern freeze, we should talk more. I appreciate your openness and hope to reciprocate the same. I am an open book, literally actually. I published a memoir in 2016 about coming out later in life called Switching Teams. Despite the book I am a pretty private person and an introvert. Weird mix, right?

My wife passed recently from metastatic breast cancer. We had no idea she was sick until a week prior. We were best friends for 17 years and together as a couple for 7. The number 17 seems to be a popular one huh? Be safe and we can connect when you get back from your trip. DW"

New Dawn. New Day. New Life

She later told me she said, *"Oh shit!"* out loud when she read it.

"Leaving the tundra first thing in the morning and going to be a rough morning, my son is heading back to Japan tomorrow. He is in the Navy. Always hard saying see ya later to him. He is my one and only. Hope you had a positive week. Dawn"

"Goodbyes are hard. Hope your time with him was amazing and that the tundra is kind as you vacate it. I want to be up front with you and make sure that you know where I am at right now. I truly am looking for friendship and to meet new people. I am not ready to even begin to think about being in anything other than a friendship. If you are okay with that then I hope we can find a way to meet or talk and cultivate that first. I am new to the online thing and apparently it is a faux pas to be on there and not looking to fall in love in 2 days and move in together LOL. Lesbians are so difficult.

If you are killing time and interested in knowing more about me, I have a blog on my website. I know you have also experienced a loss and maybe we can help each other maneuver this shitty and tough time. Anyway, sorry for rambling. I will be sending some good thoughts for a sweet parting with your son and safe travels home from the tundra. Peace, DW"

"FYI, I downloaded it and I am reading it now. Hope Holiday was not too rough on you. Dawn"

We still joke about how adamant we were with her "long time, if ever, to get over the hurt" and my own "there is no way I can think about anything other than friendship" via email.

Moving Through

We exchanged phone numbers when it was clear neither of us were serial killers. Texting followed which brought to light even more coincidences. We discovered she was from the same small town in New York where my ex-husband grew up. She knew who he was. In fact, he and her ex-wife were on the same little league team when they were twelve. The exes also went to the same high school. I told her the name of her ex before she could tell me. Her ex was the only girl in little league back in the day. I heard her name often because of her athletic talents and included photos of the team when I made my ex a 40th birthday scrapbook.

We drove the same color, make, and model car. We spent time texting and talking on the phone learning about each other, crying at times, and laughing. It felt amazing to laugh. Before we even met face to face, we were friends. We listened, advised, and just let each other be. I understood the drama unfolding with her soon to be ex-wife and surprisingly enough she fully understood and was unshaken by my widow status.

During our first conversation she wondered why I had not asked about my book. I assumed she downloaded it when I told her about it. Nope. From the way her email read, I thought she downloaded it after learning of it from me. Four months earlier, she downloaded a bunch of self-help books to make sense of the drama unfolding in her own marriage. While searching, my book appeared as a suggestion on Amazon and she downloaded it. She confessed to reading pieces intermittently as she dealt with her personal chaos. She also came out after being married to a man.

New Dawn. New Day. New Life

Soon after we began communicating, she realized my face looked familiar. Then she saw my name and realized I was the author of the book she had downloaded. She knew of me months before we ever connected on the dating site. From that point on, she put the book down and wanted to get to know me in person and said she would read it eventually.

We grilled each other about likes, dislikes, and food favorites and found we had similar tastes and opinions on many topics. Our similarities far outweighed our differences. Our career path in sales as well as our love of sports and competition were just the tip of the iceberg. For fun, we made a game of trying to find anything which would indicate being in each other's lives was a bad idea.

If you are keeping track, the universe is three for three.

Before we met in person, we exchanged long emails explaining how fragile we were and how there would be no expectations of anything other than lunch and a fun trip to the zoo. We agreed to meet at a restaurant but ended up meeting at my house. I wanted to impress her with my cooking skills. Honestly, I wanted to show her right out of the gate I was a better cook than she claimed to be.

While our friendship was growing, I stayed grounded and present. Meeting someone new so soon after losing a spouse was a slippery slope. For every reason, opinion, or whispering I risked subjecting myself to, there was a little voice whispering to me about keeping promises. Add timing to the list of things which I have failed to control in my life. I checked in with my inner circle and made sure everyone understood I was not avoiding my grief by dating and cautiously proceeding with friendship as the goal. My intention was to be open to the universe and see what happened.

FIRST DATE

I watched her walk up the drive and as the front door opened my dog was the first to greet her. She grabbed her collar to keep her from running out. When our eyes met, I saw her smile and most amazing dimple. My only thought was "there you are." It was an amazing first moment. I gave her the nickel tour and we laughed about the dog liking her already.

The conversations leading up to our meeting were filled with one upping and talking smack about our "game." Well, lack of game since we had both been in long term relationships. On paper we were a great match and in person we knocked it out of the park. The cautious approach went out the window when I kissed her forty-five minutes after she walked in the door. It was short and sweet. In my mind I won.

She later admitted being upset she did not initiate the first kiss. She hates losing. Our friendly competition was just beginning. In the dog world, we would be called alpha dogs. Trying to one up each other is a daily occurrence and we knew this would be the one obstacle we would have to contend with if our relationship progressed past friends.

Lunch was served and we left for the zoo. She drove. Our annual family pass had not expired yet and I casually mentioned on the way she would have to pretend she was Yvette if they asked her name. She did not flinch. We wandered around the zoo and held hands for hours. Before we left, we sat on a bench by the front entrance watching the merry-go-round.

I leaned against her and felt like I could breathe. We both shared our desire to never get married again and our plan for relearning how to be an individual after being in a relationship. Who knew that our quest to find ourselves would bring us together?

If someone told us we would find love with the first person we met on an online dating site, they would have been laughed at. Not us. Cautious, careful, and calculating people do not jump into relationships and certainly not after the losses we'd just experienced. No way. If ever. Our own shock and disbelief were the topic of many conversations early on.

How could this be happening? Without any clear answers, and each of us feeling we had nothing left to lose, we just went with it. We ignored our instincts to guard ourselves and proceeded with open hearts. The speed with which we met and became friends was not surprising. She is an amazing woman. We just clicked. The comfort and peace we extended to one another was unexplainable. Our story is as unbelievable as the situations we faced prior to meeting one another.

Life became both a mourning of love lost, and a celebration of love found. More on that later. Fortunately, my Dawn is in the same boat and understands. Our journey together has been equal parts rising and falling.

Individually, we are healing our respective wounds which makes for some interesting days. Separately, and together, we have been dealing with our losses and not always operating as our best selves as we move through. Triggers about our old relationships trip us up and we are mindful of our past experiences as we build a life together.

Despite those off days, we continue to define love as an action and way of being. It is a verb, not a noun. How we are is love. Whatever that looks like. Love is just as much frustration, impatience, and some ugly moments as it is laughing, joyous, and tender ones. Love is also a choice. A decision. A commitment to work through individual flaws and patterns which negatively affect each other.

Reality teaches us both that you cannot have one without the other. Yin and yang. History has shown life to be a mix of good and bad days as well as a celebration of possibilities. It is hard to maintain your bearings when life has been turned upside down for any reason. Insert whatever trouble may be playing out in your life here. There is where the work begins. Sorry. You saw this one coming, right? How you navigate the waves determines the outcome. Off to work we go.

On a good day, moving forward looks effortless and feels light. But what happens when getting out of our own way proves to be a challenge? It happens daily. Love is work. Growing is work. Hi ho hi ho. Our friendship sustains us on those sloppy emotional days.

We are fortunate to have found one another as we limp along our way and build a life together. Love is the glue that keeps us sane when one of us is losing their shit or triggered. Between the two of us, we bring an entire plane full of baggage to the party and some of our suitcases really do not go well together. Our similarities mitigate our differences, but love is our peacemaker.

Love is the thread that allows forgiveness and brings contrition when one of us forgets who we are. Love is also the fuel in the tank that allows us to focus on what is possible while letting go of what was. Our brand of love is a safe place to land as well as a reinforced shelter to work through the anger, hurt, disappointment, and the many twists our lives have taken. Without this safety and security, we would both be lost and consumed by our inner voice and internal garbage.

Why is this important? In the spirit of truth and authenticity, what follows is dedicated to everyone who feels like they must edit themselves for the sake of other people.

Conversations about beginning a relationship with someone new were judged harshly by some. Many were not aware of the promise I made to Yvette to let someone love me. I agreed after she threatened to haunt me if I planned on moping around the rest of my life. I just happened to have an opportunity to keep the promise sooner than expected.

On March 10, 2019 "My Dawn" and I got married. The whole shebang. A beautiful venue, amazing caterer, fantastic photographer, videographer, incredible DJ, and wedding planner type of wedding. We wrestled with the theme "Third time is the charm" but thought better of it.

Celebrating us privately is easy. Publicly, the shadow of relationships past creates hesitation. While not at the forefront of my mind most days, there are moments when I catch myself feeling conflicted. I questioned whether I could be happy and love again and if it diminished what Yvette and I had. Despite permission from her, I still guarded myself from judgement.

My inner circle reassured me it was what she wanted for me. My head knew the truth, but my heart still needed reassurance. The big wedding was my idea. Typically, I am not one to make a fuss, but I wanted this fuss. Our fuss. Finding Dawn, falling in love, and sharing life together was worthy of a 75-person fuss.

Our paths crossed at just the right time and our journey is still unfolding. As we moved closer to the wedding day, we were mindful of the past yet committed to forging our own way.

Summoning the courage to trust, love, and heal is our primary goal every day. Even though the DJ list of "do not play songs" was longer than our request list, we were excited. Our wedding was one way to affirm that happiness after loss is possible as well as the many forms love takes throughout a lifetime.

Even though we are now married, we still shake our heads and wonder how we got so lucky and marvel at how the universe manages to bring us what we need when we are ready to receive it. Unexpected love is a gift. Loving someone new after losing a spouse to death or divorce is work. For as wonderful as our lives have been since we found each other, there is a flip side.

We are different people than we were with our previous spouses. Time, circumstance, and life smacked us right between the eyes. Neither of us were prepared for the end of our marriages yet together we have created a space where we are free to grieve and mourn those losses. Some days we argue, stumble, and run head on into our respective triggers.

Taking care of what happens in between our ears privately and as a couple is not negotiable. For every bright moment there is a high likelihood one of us was in tears at some point during the day. Despite the growing pains, we are fortunate to be with someone who understands and offers support when those dark moments pop up.

Building this new relationship has simultaneously taken place as I have moved through the grief of losing my wife. Emotions are unavoidable. In fact, the gears of life are greased by our emotions. Paying attention to feelings and releasing them is how light reaches through the sad or dark moments. Finding a partner who can withstand the waves has been a great comfort.

Opening myself up to the possibilities ahead was exciting and terrifying. I have struggled mightily to stay in the present moment. It is easy to get stuck thinking about the past and how things were before everything changed. Building the new while honoring the old is an art not a science. Our family has grown closer, expanded, and is fantastic in ways we never saw coming.

Each day that passes is a new opportunity for healing. It is a great feat to keep this mindset handy on the hard days. Looking at it this way has helped create space for a new relationship, outlook, and growth. Moving through the pain and experiencing new joy, love, and hope for the future is an interesting space. Learning that the capacity for both extremes to exist at the same time was strange at first, but now feels familiar.

The ability to bounce back and keep moving forward is not a given. Digging deep and taking a long hard look at every angle and curve includes brutal honesty and squashing the fear of what could happen or concern over what other people think. When things are rough, it is okay to rest a bit, but never give up.

As you maneuver through your own winding road, do not be afraid to feel the hard things and admit when you are struggling. Resist the temptation to retreat and shrink down when choosing yourself and joy is not met with applause from everyone else.

A wedding is not necessary to begin letting go of whatever hold the past, present, or future may have over you. Decide. Decide again and again. Be, love, and learn to be content with what is as you move toward what will be.

Where there is loss of any kind, there is change. Whether physical, mental, emotional, or spiritual, the source is irrelevant. Let go or be dragged is a favorite mantra and helped give perspective to my grief journey. Accepting this has been one of the most liberating and freeing revelations. Just be. Who knew?

As you roll through the changes and mark time in your world, please remember to be gentle and kind to yourself along the journey. Being too rigid will slow your roll. Instead, try embracing the idea that you are exactly where you are supposed to be regardless of the chaos swirling or uncertainty you are facing. Keep going forward. It is the direction home.

11 - FORWARD IS THE DIRECTION HOME

Are there any out there who like being uncomfortable? Anyone? Didn't think so. We all have different thresholds, triggers, and definitions of the word uncomfortable. Companies make millions coming up with ways to help make us more comfortable. Eradicating all physical, mental, emotional, or spiritual woes is an impossible task but shifting how we view discomfort may be able to offer some relief.

There are many approaches to soothing ourselves when discomfort strikes. Our personality, life experience, and mindset are all factors influencing how well we handle the chaotic or unexpected moments in our lives. How we respond when we are feeling uncomfortable plays a significant role in how quickly we move through it.

Although you may not always have a say in what happens, you always have a choice when it comes to how you respond. Let's look at the most popular responses. Avoidance. Recoiling from things that make us squirm is a natural reaction. Thank you fight or flight.

No one I know would happily run full speed, butt ass naked, and jump on a pile of vertically placed knives. Sidestepping may seem easier in the moment but pressing the pause button or pretending like something unpleasant does not exist only compounds the problem.

The flip side of this coin includes immersing yourself in the discomfort and becoming consumed by it. Also known as the get stuck and suck the joy out of life approach. If the goal is to give fear a full access backstage pass to your thinking and emotions, then this is the method of choice. However, it is not really a sexy choice is it?

A third approach includes examining the cause, feeling the emotions, and moving through it. Is this hard? Yes. Is it fun? Not always. Is it necessary to eventually feel peace? Yes. While this may sound very similar to the get stuck approach, there is a big difference between stopping for a moment to process and feeding the monster to the point of exhaustion.

Option number three sounds great but this approach takes patience, wisdom, and a willingness to stop fighting the things we cannot control. It requires the ability to separate how something feels in the moment from the reality of the situation. Also included in this approach is letting go of the idea that all discomfort is negative or bad.

If your life has not gone as planned, raise your hand. Take heart in the fact you are in the majority. Even though things may have unfolded unexpectedly in your world, the simple fact that you are reading this means you are still here. Despite the failed plans, or twists and turns, you are still here. And without even knowing it, you have been handling your shit the entire time.

The journey is not about surviving but about living our best lives possible. The energy required to just get by and survive is enormous and much greater than spending the time necessary understanding why we react and behave like we do. In order to move past those unexpected or deeply engrained behaviors, we must begin within ourselves.

CHANGE

Moving forward means dealing with change. Change can be as small as switching laundry detergents and needing time to adjust to the new smell on your clothes. It can also be bigger than anything we imagine and happen without warning. Unexpected changes are never a picnic but changes which happen with advance warning can feel just as unsettling. Which is easier? None of it for most of us.

The summer I dropped off my oldest son for his first year of college brought changes galore. Despite having an entire summer to ready ourselves for his departure, no amount of preparation or advanced notice stopped me from bawling the entire ride home and for the two weeks that followed, give or take.

Moving Through

This was a marking point in time for not only him, but for our family as well. If I am being honest, and possibly a little overly dramatic, it felt like the beginning of the end. From that moment on, we expected his time in our home would be limited to summers and holidays.

After a year of college, his plans changed. Instead of finishing his degree in finance, he decided to become an electrician and moved back home. He traded the college life for working full time and beginning classes to become a journeyman in a career he decided was a better fit for him. This kid is one of my heroes and the poster child for fearless living.

He listened to his inner voice and spent little time wondering what would be lost if he quit college. He looked ahead to what he had to gain with his decision. Instead of ruminating over what not having a four-year degree would mean for his future, he took steps to create a secure future with a high demand career. Ballsy if you ask me. Proud momma moment. He made the choice despite the objections of his father. His "forward is the direction home" moment was bold and brave.

What is the difference between someone who is successful at dodging and rolling with things as they happen and those who get jammed up and stuck? Life shifts, and we must adjust.

Life is a series of moments which require quick feet and nimble hands. Being able to dodge when life weaves requires skill and fortitude. High fives for those who are experts in navigating change. For the rest of us, I can empathize. I, too, have felt paralyzed by fear and overwhelmed when events outside of my control play out. Other times it is smooth sailing. The goal is not eliminating change but learning how to be flexible during changes.

While we cannot control the when, where, how, why, or who of change, we can choose how we react and respond to it. Baby steps or leaps. The choice is yours. Start small and build from there. Think carefully about the pros and cons of situations and stay grounded in hope that not all change has to affect us in a negative way. Viewing change in this light allows space to create a plan to handle whatever comes our way.

One of the biggest reasons we fight change is our inability to see what there is to gain instead of what we are giving up. When my son left, it was difficult to see past what was lost, namely my oldest son's presence in our house and daily life. The last thing on my mind was the potential gain for not only him, but us. Our loss was his gain.

Being able to look at the possibility change offers rather than the deficits is not easy. Reframing thinking is easier when we remind ourselves how boring life would be if everything stayed the same. Eliminating change, expected and unexpected, is a feat not yet mastered by any walking on this earth.

When we believe we can rise above whatever is thrown our way, big or small, life is good. It takes time and practice to learn to think in a new way. Progress may seem slow, but even the simple decision to briefly consider what the upside may be is a step in the right direction. In those moments, you may be surprised to find that you feel energized and strong rather than stuck.

Confidence and fortitude are like muscles and grow when we retrain our minds like gymnasts' train for their events. Life is a lot like the Olympics. We may not all be Michael Phelps in the pool, but with effort and determination we can earn our own Olympic medals in the dealing with change arena.

Making peace with change, both known and unknown, is the first step in creating a life that is not weighted down with fear and negativity. Learning to be hopeful and optimistic during the shit storms is a gift to ourselves and affords the opportunity to make it through whatever we stumble upon along our journey.

Challenge yourself to allow for the possibility of thinking about the upside. Pay attention. Look for opportunities to focus on what may be gained rather than focusing on the chaos, changes, or fact that things did not go as planned. There is no room for the negative messages and defeatist self-talk on this road.

PERFECTION TRAP

The magic happens when we give ourselves permission to stop trying to arrive at perfection. Releasing the pressure and stress associated with figuring everything out in order to be happy opens the door to peace and authentic living. This is the space where healing, self-love, authenticity, and the work begins. Forward is the direction home.

Forward is the Direction Home

In my own journey, I realized the power in stopping to catch my breath and stepping back. My most enlightening moments happened when all motion stopped, and I could hear only myself. For many years I operated under the belief that something was wrong with me. In turn, my behavior, thoughts, and emotions were affected. Backward is not the direction home.

Everything changed when I started challenging my own internal dialogue, examined the sources of doubt, and began showing the same amount of kindness to myself as I did to others. Authenticity 101 began here.

Resisting the temptation to classify ourselves as broken is the first homework assignment. The first chapter in the class textbook is titled "You Are Not Broken." Broken things require fixing. People are people, not things. Battered, weathered, worn out, or frustrated are not indicators of brokenness. They are natural feelings stemming from where you have been, the things you have experienced, and the circumstances of your life. The alternative descriptor to broken is human.

Living a "forward is the direction home" philosophy begins with ourselves. Learning who we are, and who we are not, is a critical piece of the puzzle. Tackling fear, finding courage, and getting our minds right is how we find our bearings home.

One of the best days after the cancer diagnosis was the day I took Yvette to Playa Linda Beach. This was no ordinary beach. Her words tell the story best. It was truly a shining example of "forward is the direction home."

Moving Through

"I thought at this time I would be recovering from surgery, or at the very least preparing for it. However, my surgeon has been called for jury duty, so Dawn and I are doing the thing we love the most. Waiting. So, while I wait, I decided to write about when we went to a nude beach. I mentioned it at the end of the last blog and thought better of it, but I have been asked about it, so I hope I make it sound as interesting as you hope it was!

I am not a prude although I am very modest. My wife on the other hand finds clothing to be an annoying necessity of social acceptance. One of the things on her bucket list was to go to the nude beach at Canaveral National Seashore. Also known as Playa Linda Beach.

We attempted it earlier this year, but it was too crowded, and we ended up on the beach with all the regular people in their bathing suits. A few days after my cancer diagnosis, I awoke one morning to my wife smiling and asking if I was up for an adventure.

At that point anything sounded better than just sitting around staring at each other in shock." What do I wear?" was, of course, my first question. "You don't need to worry about that!" was her response. Oh boy, I had a feeling...

The ride to the beach was beautiful, a perfect fall day in Florida. Deep blue skies, puffy white clouds and a warm breeze, perfect for frolicking around naked on the shore! I was a little nervous when we stepped onto the beach and wanted to find a spot that wasn't close to the other sun bathers.

We walked looking for a place to settle all the while trying to decide between us what the proper etiquette was for interacting...do you look?

Avert the eyes? Act like everyone is clothed? I felt like I was lost in that old fairy tale The Emperor's New Clothes.

I noticed a group of men, standing bare ass naked, talking to each other while their man parts were mere inches away from each other. Funny, I thought, if they were in Walmart or at the grocery store, they would not dare be in that close of a proximity to one another.

Secretly, we both were rooting for their parts to accidentally touch just to see what happened next. Can you imagine? Naked apparently was the new normal. At that moment, we declared hence to forthwith this section of sand to be called "Sausage Beach".

We finally found a spot with a little space around us and set up our chairs. Almost immediately an older man came walking towards us, parts swaying in the wind, to ask if we wanted to take a walk down the beach with him. Really? Dude, I just got here. Give me a break! And…NO! We must have been impressive as we still had our clothes on! Gave new meaning to the word wrinkled, I mean, welcome wagon.

It wasn't long before Dawn went for it. I dared to take off the top of my suit. You know, ease into it. Not two minutes later my amazing wife was completely nude and literally dancing around her chair in the sun. In the spirit of unity, I admit I quickly followed "suit" without the dancing, no dancing. Can't dance topless, someone may get hurt.

For the first and only time in my 47 years, I sat on the beach bare ass nekkid! It was one of the most liberating feelings I have ever had. Funny how the news of breast cancer and the reality of living without breasts will loosen up any stuffy old rules you have lived by or better yet, been constrained by for your whole life.

Who cares if my boobs and girly bits were out for the world to see! Take a good look boys and girls, it's the farewell tour for my pain in the ass tatas! My only regret is that I didn't do this years ago. I didn't even wince when Dawn brought out the video camera to record my reaction to my newfound freedom! What the hell ever!

We sat there watching stark-naked people swim in the surf, chat with each other, walk the beach, pick up shells, and just enjoy their liberty. I will confess that I did look away when the guys bent over to pick up shells...really, no one needs to see that, lesbian or not. Some things cannot be unseen.

Adding to the fun was trying to suppress hysterical laughter while watching a short roundish man attempt to get out of the circular spider net bungee cord chair he was sitting in. You cannot make this stuff up. Getting caught up in that mess could have left a permanent injury. We were rooting for him to succeed. Honestly. Can you imagine the 911 call? Anyone see my cell phone?

After a few hours it was time to go. We would have stayed longer, but we did not factor in the rate that skin never touched by the sun would burn or that in our excitement to leave the house we would forget to pack the sunscreen. Plus, sand was getting in places it did not belong despite our best efforts to prevent it.

Before we left, I stopped at the restroom...barf...don't ever use a public restroom at the beach. Dawn, taking heed of my mistake, disappeared into the palmetto scrub. This is probably too much information, but that's how we roll in Waters Land. Hey, you asked...

Forward is the Direction Home

Ironically, as I was writing this, the doctor's office called with a surgery date. No more waiting. Boobmageddon is upon us"

The day at the beach was among my all-time favorites. Freedom from our baggage was lapping the shore like the waves. Forward is the direction home. In the wake of Yvette's death, I lacked any direction. The be fearless chick was terrified. The tide turned and I wondered if I would be able to take my own advice about dealing with fear.

12 - HELLO ANXIETY

The canvas which is life begins the day we are born and ends the day we take our last breath. Being married to an artist taught me the beauty of art is not in the finished product, but rather in the process of creating it. But what happens when fear colors our canvas and threatens to knock the art off our walls?

ANXIETY AND DEPRESSION.

Do you remember the last time you were free from all worry or anxiety? I do. It was December 2010 when I realized I was a lesbian. As unbelievable as it sounds, the least anxious time in my life was immediately after coming out.

Least anxious being defined as zero anxiety. Zip. Zilch. Nada. Despite the stress, change, logistics, and circumstances, I experienced peace. I credit the miracle of survival mode. My lack of anxiety during that time may have defied explanation but was not permanent.

Hello Anxiety

Moments of feeling afraid and unsure about our lives or the world in general is common. We worry about how our choices will affect those around us, if we are eating enough fiber, making the cut with our peers, or if we turned off the coffee pot.

The list is endless and encompasses more than worrying about things we have control over. What about the things we feel powerless to change or have no control over? Elections, world peace, being a homosexual, and the choices of others which may directly impact us are a few worth noting. Worry and anxiety are similar. Both are fear based and impact thoughts and feelings. However, they are not always the same thing.

Worry is fretting about if your kids will make straight A's on their report card. Anxiety comes out of nowhere and feels like an elephant sitting on your chest. In my case, it was leaving for school in the morning when I was a young child and being convinced that my family would be dead when I got home.

My "friend" anxiety and I go way back but I did not know its name until I was a young adult. Dealing with it felt like being forced to take your bratty little sister with you wherever you went. Sometimes it was not a big deal and other times was completely aggravating.

Only after I got diagnosed with an anxiety disorder did I understand what was responsible for my sudden panic and fear when nothing was happening. It is not something I wish on anyone and genuinely empathize with my fellow soldiers in the anxious army.

Moving Through

Being diagnosed with Generalized Anxiety Disorder in my twenties was both a relief and an annoyance. Anxious thoughts are unpredictable, notoriously irrational, and just wait for an opportunity to mess up my day. It pretty much does what it wants, when it wants. Bastard. My work begins when, not if, it happens.

Over time, I learned to manage and even embrace this frustrating part of who I am. Some days are better than others. In the rough moments, reaching into the mental health toolbox does not always guarantee an easy fix. I may be an expert in having anxiety, but I am also an expert in forgetting how to push through when I feel afraid. Anyone else with me on this one?

I was not under any delusion that coming out would completely eradicate the anxiety. I just enjoyed the break. Truthfully, there is no fix for getting rid of anxiety. The week Yvette was in the hospital, I spent my energy fighting the anxiety. There are only ways to mitigate and cope with it after it is rolling. It may feel impossible to find peace when everything feels off kilter, but that feeling is the anxiety talking and not the truth. While there may not be a cure, there are ways to make it less paralyzing.

A trip to the beach sounds relaxing, right? Not always. A simple excursion to the beach with Yvette and your youngest son should be fun. However, I was anxious about going but still went. Little victories. Finding peace in those anxious moments can take every ounce of energy present. It is exhausting and frustrating. Trying to fight it only makes it worse.

Hello Anxiety

I had a choice to make. Be miserable or find peace. For me, it meant focusing on the present moment and getting much needed time away from work and the responsibilities of everyday life. It meant breathing deeply and putting my attention on watching my son boogie board in the waves. It meant getting out of my own head long enough to be reminded how much I love watching my boys have fun. The joy in that moment was louder than whatever anxious thoughts or feelings were happening in my brain.

Fear comes in many shapes and forms. None are immune to feeling fear and not all fear is unhealthy. Fear itself exists to protect us from threats to our safety and lives. The silver lining here is that even though we cannot eliminate fear from our lives, we all have the ability within to manage worry, anxiety, and fear.

Knowing this gives even the twitchiest among us hope. Thankfully, there are many ways to go about the business of nipping worry and anxiety in the bud. Some choose meditation, others choose medication. Discovering the method that works best is unique to every individual.

If you are struggling, ask for help from your family, friends, or a therapist. Talk about it. Do not be ashamed or hide your battle from the world. Trust that you are not your anxious thoughts and that dealing with it, though challenging, is not an impossible task. If one approach does not work, keep trying to find the one that does.

If you know someone who is anxious and have a difficult time understanding why they cannot just stop worrying or feeling anxious, learn what anxiety is and what it is not. Be sympathetic to the fact that anxious people have anxiety about their anxiety and how it impacts not only their lives, but the lives of those around them.

While we may not understand what we have not personally experienced, we certainly can do our best to offer kindness and love to those who are suffering with physical, mental, or emotional baggage. The bags we carry may be a variety of colors, brands, sizes, and have different points of origin, but the road we travel is the same.

After reading one of my blogs about anxiety, Yvette was inspired to contribute her perspective on life with an anxious person.

"This week my wife wrote a blog about living with anxiety. I am a professional photographer who would rather take pictures than write down my thoughts. However, I thought it might be worthwhile to share my thoughts about what it is like to love someone who has Generalized Anxiety Disorder. It is not always easy. It can be confusing, lonely, frustrating and stressful. Sometimes it feels like wandering through a maze where neither of us can seem to find the exit.

Sounds like fun doesn't it? The truth is, it can be a hell of a ride, but don't run away or stop reading just yet. I am here to offer some hope and a few reminders that have helped me learn about my wife, and more importantly about me.

I have known my wife for fifteen years. As we became closer, I saw how this wonderfully confident and funny woman could also be crippled by her anxiety at times. If you met Dawn for the first time, you may not be able to tell she is anxious. For years I have watched her quietly fight the anxiety and take steps to help keep it at bay and not let fear win. She is strong, determined, and very aware of her limitations but sometimes the mother fucker wins.

Sometimes she gets very quiet and does what we call around our house "going in her head." As friends, I knew this was part of how she copes with her anxiety. As her wife, I have had to remind myself that she is not shutting me out when she is dealing with anxious thoughts. I guess the best piece of advice I can give is to not take it personally. Reminder: It's not about you.

I recently read an article which labeled anxious people as moody, as if their mood was a choice. What bullshit. My wife is the least moody person I have ever known. However, there are times when I do see what I call a "shift" in her demeanor, attention, or body language. One moment she is fine and the next moment the shift happens.

It's not being moody, it's anxiety. She goes into her head to cope and manage whatever is pinging. The most helpful thing in those moments is to give her some space to breathe and remind her that she is not the anxiety. Reminder: Who we are is separate from what we deal with.

Anxious thoughts are irrational and the person with the anxious thoughts KNOWS IT. Pointing it out or expecting them to just stop thinking it will not help at all, not one bit. So for the love of all that is holy please don't say those things, unless you want to get punched. (By me, I will punch you). Reminder: Expecting someone with anxiety to stop feeling anxious is like telling someone with epilepsy to stop having a seizure.

Moving Through

Anxiety loves to ruin plans. Going places and doing things is never set in stone. Sometimes what was fine yesterday is not fine today. There is no rhyme or reason to it. There have been times when we decided to go somewhere, and Dawn just could not do it. Thanks anxiety. And by that, I mean fuck you anxiety. To pressure her or give her a hard time would only add to the stress she is already feeling, which is not kind or loving. I love her more than the plans we made.

Here is the thing: it's not that the plans you made aren't important. It's not that spending time with family and friends is not important. It's not about being uninterested in a night out. It is about the anxiety making it nearly impossible to do it. When this happens, no one feels worse about it than Dawn does. Reminder: Be flexible and choose love.

Most people know a lot more about Dawn than they do about me. I am the behind the scenes person and usually behind the lens. So I will tell you something about myself. I LOVE to talk. I can chat for hours about serious issues or about nothing important. I ask a lot of questions. I am always trying to understand what is happening.

Dawn, however, doesn't like to talk as much as I do, especially when she's anxious. Sometimes too many questions and conversation about the anxiety causes the anxiety to increase. The question "are you ok?" does not help at all. I know, I have asked. She is not ok and has told me many times, in her outside voice, how dumb asking that question is in those moments. I have learned the value in saying "just breathe".

No one is more aware of how confusing and debilitating the anxiety is than my wife. Talking about it frustrates her and interrupts the work she is trying to do to settle her brain. The anxiety passes more quickly when she is not feeling like a loser for not being able to explain what is happening. Don't add to the mix. Reminder: Silence is golden. (You can thank my therapist for this one, Dawn certainly does.)

I'm going to let you in on a Waters' secret. Writing the book *Switching Teams*, weekly blogging, and opening her life for the world to see and sometimes scrutinize are the most anxiety producing things she does. It is not always a pretty sight. In fact it seems masochistic to me at times. But she does it anyway. Sharing her story forces her to get out of her comfort zone and face her own fears. I know her message of being authentic and choosing peace has been extremely encouraging to many. It has helped me to be more understanding, supportive, and patient as her wife and life partner.

Don't get me wrong. I am not suggesting taking one for the team or just sucking it up and dealing with it. The person with anxiety is responsible for their part as well. I know I can't make the anxiety go away, but I can support her by doing what I can to be aware of situations I know might trigger her anxiety. If we had a Waters crest it would be inscribed with "Handle Your Shit". When I see the effort on her end, it is easier for me to be patient and understanding when I see my wife struggling or feeling overwhelmed.

Encourage your partner to get help if they are struggling with anxiety. Asking for help is a brave first step toward self-care. My last reminder is the most important. We all have our own mountains to climb and the way a relationship looks depends on how both people "handle their shit". Difficult moments test relationships, but also can make them stronger. Just because it is hard, does not mean it is not good, or even *amazing. The struggles are what bring you closer, help build trust, and deepen your love for each other. Which is the point, isn't it?"*

For someone who preferred photographs over words, she nailed it.

13 - FEAR IS A LIAR

Fear is a liar we seldom call out on its deception. Fear fools us into believing discomfort is something to be avoided at all costs. Waging a war on the presence of fear in our minds is a frightening undertaking. Negotiating with the terrorist in our own thoughts is futile. Loosening the stronghold it has on our lives is critical to our personal growth, happiness, and well-being.

Fear is an asshole and it gets its own chapter. Rightfully so. Fear exists to protect us from danger. It keeps us safe under dangerous conditions and is a very important part of our internal make up, yet it can serve to cause problems in our life when we let it rule every aspect of how we live. Fear skews our perception and convinces us things are not how they seem.

It can infiltrate every corner of life and makes every day seem scary. We all have fears we must deal with. Luckily enough, fear is my number one nemesis. Reflecting on how fear, anxiety, and worry have colored my world, I have reached expert level in understanding how it operates. Knowing how it operates is nice but learning to choose freedom and courage when afraid is where the rubber meets the road.

In a perfect world, its sole purpose is to protect us from perceived threats. Fight or flight response is a chemical process in our brain that kicks in when a danger is present. It is an innate biological reaction which results when unsafe situations arise. As humans, living a fear free life would be dangerous and completely insane. How else would we know to run from a bear or move out of the way of moving traffic?

Our reaction to scary things may be encoded in our DNA, but it can also be a learned behavior. In fact, most is learned. Ouch. I know. Our reactions to everyday life can inadvertently teach our kids to be afraid. Many irrational fears are just moments when our brain overcorrected, invented, or inflated a perceived threat. Learned fears are what stop us cold and prevent us from achieving inner peace and happiness.

The short list includes the fear of rejection, abandonment, failure, inadequacy, commitment, intimacy, or even success. How many times does the fear of hurting others stop us from acting in our own best interests? How often do we feel like our efforts are not enough? Being afraid is contagious and can be found at the heart of chaos in our relationships, families, and lives.

Years of self-introspection and analysis, hundreds of self-help books, and mountains of research on the topic has enlightened me about what fear is, what it is not, and what things I can do to keep it from running the show. Yay me. However, knowing about it and learning how to overcome it are two totally different things. Boo me. Determination, perseverance, and mindfulness are prerequisites for the task.

My perception of the world was viewed through a filter of fear. Shifting the lens teaches us that without fear there would be no opportunities to be fearless. Looking at it in this light is less frightening. I fight fear every day. How about you? Being a parent is fear central. Safety, health, bullies, and doing everything to prevent suffering creates fear.

Hardly a day passes in our house when the subject of fear is not addressed in one form or another. Not only did Yvette and I fight anxiety, but two out of four of the kids also struggle with it. Worry and fear go hand in hand. Although there is no simple solution or pill which can instantly evict fear from our beings, there are some suggestions which will help move past what keeps us from living a peace filled life.

1-*Make a list:* Making lists helps expose the roots of the weed so it can be pulled up from the ground. Some prefer avoiding their fears as a means of coping. While effective in the short term, it can make things worse in the long term. The act of writing out our fears is therapeutic on many levels.

What are you afraid of? You must name it before you can do anything about it. Grab a piece of paper and write it down. This is the hardest part of the process. Naming it serves two purposes. First, it forces us to acknowledge its presence and the impact it has on our lives. Second, it puts our negative thoughts on notice and signals a willingness to begin the work involved. As we think so shall we be. Once named, we can begin the process of evaluating alternative responses or reactions to the things in life that create the most dread.

2-*Feel your fear*: I have a love hate relationship with this one. Allowing yourself to feel the fear is like dropping 200 feet in seconds while flying over the ocean. Our natural reaction is to run, which only feeds it. Feeling the fear strips it of its power and offers evidence that this too shall pass. It is not fun, but it works. Sometimes we forget the mind is just as capable of removing fear as it is creating it.

Coming out was an exercise in facing my fears. Everything caught up with me in very short order and no other choice remained but to finally start the process of thinking and feeling my way out of the avalanche. Realizing that my operating system was flawed helped me to find the courage to shift my thinking.

3-*Put fear in its place*: My life changed when I recognized fear was running the show. My come to Jesus moment happened when my desire to live authentically was greater than any of my fears. This process looks different for each of us and varies depending on the circumstance.

Examining the impact of operating from a fearful mindset jump starts the process of embracing our authentic selves and nurturing our ability to embrace fearless living. As I have mentioned many times, the single most helpful book I have read on this subject is called Fearless Living written by Rhonda Britten. If you struggle with fear, this book will not disappoint.

As you move through your own journey, I encourage you to take one small step toward letting go of whatever may be blocking your path to peace. Be mindful of the fact that what we fear is often much worse in our heads than it will be in real life. If you are feeling especially bold and inspired, I highly recommend telling fear to fuck off as part of your plan of attack.

As the one-year anniversary approached, I took the time to continue to process and grieve but also looked ahead to the future and keeping the promises I made to Yvette. Remember, she threatened to haunt me if I didn't.

Just prior to the one-year anniversary of her death, our family moved out of a subdivision and into a rural part of town. Our family adjusted to the darkness at night and the roaming bear, coyote, and possible Chupacabra populations. Fortunately, one of us is a security guru and has outfitted our driveway and property with various motion sensors, driveway alarms, and cameras so we can be prepared.

My Dawn calls it being prepared and safe. I see it as an invitation for mistaking squirrels for bears. My youngest son has mixed feelings about the security measures in place. Early one morning we awoke to the sound of driveway alarms. He began texting asking us to look out every window to see what was there. The trash cans on the street were untouched and the place was lit up like the Las Vegas strip. But nothing was there.

Our hearts were racing, but nothing was there. I began to think about fear and, more importantly, being fearless. There it is. Broken record warning. Be fearless. Simple, right? It is not as easy as you think, but the easiest thing ever. What? Think about it. Being fearless is a choice but does not mean you are never afraid. The contrary is true. First, a story about facing fear.

One day, reaching outside of my comfort zone looked like seeing the newest movie from the Halloween syndicate at a theater. I was seven when the first one was released and believe I am among the handful of people who never saw it. The movie was gross and gory but the trailers for upcoming films were terrifying.

I remembered why I do not enjoy scary movies before the featured show even started. During one particularly creepy and jolting moment, My Dawn looked over when I jumped out of my seat. She was amused by my reaction and reminded me none of it was real. I agreed but explained that for her, and many others, that feeling is exciting. For me, it is not.

In my experience, a racing heart is anxiety running wild and something I have contended with my entire life. Historically, adrenalin rush moments are nothing more than panic attacks waiting to happen and something I have spent most of my life trying to avoid.

Fear is a healthy part of our human experience, yet many struggle to find the sweet spot between fearful and fearless living. (Raising my hand.) Finding the wisdom to balance these two extremes is more of an art than a science. Learning the difference between feeling genuine excitement and anxiety has been life changing.

I spent the year after Yvette died learning how to discern the difference between anxiety and excitement. The two feel very similar yet are very different. Being able to distinguish the difference has only been possible because of medication. Yep, I said it. After 46 years, I finally decided to try anxiety meds. Duh.

Cognitive and behavioral therapy gave me the tools I needed to manage it, but it still impacted my daily life, career, and relationships. Prior to November of 2017, my biggest fear was something happening to my best friend and wife. When she died from metastatic breast cancer within a week of the diagnosis my fear turned to grief.

Worry and anxiety about her health took up a great deal of my time for two years. When she passed, the worry and anxiety fell away. Granted I was numb, but as time went on the realization hit. Reality check number one: when you feel like there is nothing left to lose, being fearless is not as frightening. Living my worst fear and not crumbling was surprising but encouraging.

Reality check number two: sometimes being fearless is not actually being fearless at all. Many times, it means doing whatever it is that scares the hell out of us while afraid. The truth is we are wired for fear. In its purest and most primal form it is meant to protect us from harm and keep us safe. Remember fight or flight?

Facing your fears looks different for everyone. For some, just going outside is a major victory. For others, it may look like wrestling an alligator. Some try to eradicate all danger from their environments in order to keep fear away. No two people are the same in how they respond to or rise above fear.

Removing the idyllic visual of a superhero jumping from a burning building is the first step to moving through fear. Halloween season brings many opportunities to be fearless, also known as reaching beyond our comfort zones. For someone who suffers from anxiety, this time of the year can be challenging to maneuver through. Haunted houses, chainsaw-wielding deranged clowns, or the threat of zombies are not my cup of tea, but I am a work in progress.

Whether you are afraid of Michael Myers, bears, losing a loved one, the color purple, or the number thirteen is irrelevant. Sometimes we must run from the fear in order to protect ourselves. Think bear. However, most of the time our fears are rooted in feelings which may need to be addressed on a deeper level.

The fear we cannot run from is the fear which changes us when we dig deep and uncover the source. Trauma can create fear which becomes deeply engrained in our lives and affects our choices, quality of life, and ability to feel peace. Little events or things can also cause the same result.

When afraid, we are being challenged to think, react, and change. If we look at fear as an opportunity for growth, our response to it will no longer paralyze us. Taking steps to root out fear in our lives often requires help from someone who is trained, or even medication.

This is the second step to moving through fear. Do not be afraid to ask for help if fear is keeping you stuck and affecting your life in a negative way. The most fearless act any of us can engage in is the act of asking for help. Trust me. It works.

By asking for help, we choose our wellness and reclaim power over fear. Take some time to write down the areas in life where fear is rearing its head. Before you begin, take a deep breath and know that you are not alone. Choose one small step you may take to help alleviate fear in your life.

Start small and go from there. We all can move through our fears, even if it means kicking, screaming, and hulk smashing our way through. It can also mean quietly tackling the fear of saying no, changing our minds, being our authentic selves, or making decisions which might ruffle feathers. Let the idea of doing it afraid become your new best friend and watch how things change.

The moment when I decide to create something new is glorious and filled with excitement and confidence. These are my fearless moments. The adrenalin rush is fueled by my desire to help everyone understand they are enough, important, capable, and deserving of peace in their lives. In other words, I feel like Superwoman.

Writing this book forced me to think long and hard about where I am in my own journey and how to deal with my own fears. Every idea that begins with a moment of fearlessness usually results in escalating fear as the process evolves. In other words, Clark Kent shows up and takes over. Not acknowledging my own fears as they pop up has never worked out well. Who is going to care about what I have to say? What if no one reads the book? What if those who do read it hate it? Can I do this? These thoughts are my kryptonite.

Accomplishing a task requires full immersion in the details. My laser focus is on saving the city from destruction like every superhero should. Sound familiar? It is my way of trying to dodge, outsmart, or become immunized against fear. Hilarious huh? Here is the truth.

Keeping my head down and my mind on a task is a classic avoidance technique. Ring any bells? Ignoring or avoiding it guarantees the loss of my superpowers. Not dealing with doubt or fear in the moment may seem like the easier option, but it is not. Fear is a patient opportunist that will linger if it has a comfy spot to plop down in.

If ignoring the problem worked, we would all have only peace in our lives. So, what can you do when fear is stopping you from taking the next step, keeping you in a relationship that is not healthy, or robbing you of your peace?

Instead of finding ways to work around the fear, I suggest asking yourself some questions about whatever fear is holding you hostage right now. Ask yourself, "what am I afraid of?" In order to truly address the fear, you must name it. I know. Bummer. Naming your fear takes some reflection and requires an honest look within. Again. Bummer.

Unfortunately, you cannot skip this step. Sometimes it may be a fear of failure. Other times it may be a fear of change. The fear of not being good enough or being alone are also popular. Once you name the fear, the work can begin to move through it. Notice, I said move through it.

Naming the fear does not take away the feelings or strip it of its perceived power. However, it does move our brains in a direction that allows us to begin to deal with it. This is where the work begins. Many methods and approaches to handling fear exist. I look at fear like the phone booth Clark Kent uses to transform into Superman.

Once inside the phone booth, there are three choices available. Option one is to shut the door and give in to the overwhelming and paralyzing feelings that fear brings. You can sit in the phone booth watching life happen through the glass. It seems protected and safe, but the air is thick and there is not much room to move around or get comfortable.

Option two is to open the door and consider what taking the next step would look like. Naming the fear happens in this space. Standing up and feeling the fresh air move past your face signals your brain that you are ready. It may take a minute, months, or many moons, but here is where the willingness to decide what to do about the fear and the courage to do it is born.

Option three is to grab your cape, take a deep breath, and creep, crawl, or walk out the door. This may seem crazy or like an impossible choice. It is both and neither at the same time. Also ask yourself, "what is the worst that can happen?" When fear is jacking us up, our imaginations are notorious for overestimating the worst-case scenarios. When I came out to my husband, I was convinced he was going make me pack my bags, throw me out on the street, and leave immediately. He didn't. He would never have done that, but my fear caused me to abandon every sane thought in my head. Fear is a liar.

Calling out fear for the liar that it is paves the way for courage and reason. Feeling afraid is an emotion every human being experiences in their lifetime. However, fear is not the only emotion or feeling we are capable of. Joy, peace, love, contentment, happiness, and hundreds more positive feelings are also fantastic options. Learning to navigate through fear is the most beautiful way to ensure balanced and healthy living. Give yourself permission to feel whatever you need to feel in order to face your fear. It is not always a pretty sight and sometimes feels worse before it feels better.

Trust yourself. Talk about how you are feeling and do not let the opinions of others cloud your journey. Grab that notepad again. Spend some time thinking about what you would do if you were not afraid. Be your own superhero. Know that you are so much greater than what fear says you are.

14 - COURAGE

Adversity comes in many shapes and sizes. It does not discriminate nor care if we are prepared for it. Most adversity is unexpected and usually happens at the worst possible moment. If you are among the lucky few who have never faced any challenges in life, you can stop reading now. What follows won't interest you.

The message for those dealing with adversity is simple. You absolutely will make it through. I promise. Before shaking your head in disbelief, hear me out. In my experience, there is a direct relationship between how we react to challenges and our ability to find peace. Adverse situations feel like a bucket of ice water being dumped on our heads. Our reactions to the cold water vary. Cold water will awaken some and cripple others.

What makes some better able to deal with pain or struggle than others? Our response to events we may face is determined by our background, experience, and personality. Even the most resilient people have "crawl under a rock and give up" moments.

Fortitude is defined as courage in pain or adversity. Courage is seldom the first thought when circumstances escalate out of control. Choosing fortitude while in the spiral allows us to handle anything that comes our way, if we believe that we can. Without this belief, we are left powerless in our circumstances.

There were many difficult and ugly days after I came out and after Yvette died. Ugly may be an understatement. How was I supposed to brave this storm when I could not stop throwing up or crying about what I had done to my family? How was I going to get over losing my best friend and spouse? I was a wreck. The adversity emerging from each situation added layers of guilt, sadness, and grief. Only after wearing myself out was I able to find the courage to begin putting one foot in front of the other.

Our perception of what brave looks like does not always match what we have been taught or shown. Firemen and police officers are heroic and brave. Their work requires great courage. Their brand of bravery is often what we expect the successful handling of adversity to look like. Our heroism usually looks like nothing like running in to a burning building or a high-speed chase.

We are born with an abundance of bravery and courage. Responding to and rising above adversity is an opportunity to call upon the strength, courage, and bravery we all have within. The most courageous became so because life tossed situations at them which forced them to become brave. Practice makes perfect.

Remembering this during a tsunami is the problem. Bravery often looks like controlled chaos and requires letting go of fear and choosing to do things afraid. It means stepping back, remembering our will is stronger than any fear, and adopting bravery over despair.

Why is it easier to see and celebrate the courage in others but become paralysed when in similar situations? There is something powerful about watching someone rise above pain or adversity. However, the lesson is not complete until we learn how to push past our own obstacles. Examples abound. Learning to draw strength from others will strengthen our fortitude muscles.

Drawing inspiration from others in our most vulnerable moments allows us to defer to the big picture. It also creates space for the belief that we can overcome and adapt to changing circumstances. After Yvette was diagnosed with cancer, I asked her if she would let me take more pictures of her. I took her yes to mean making videos as well. She was not thrilled but did it despite her objection to being in front of cameras. She would do anything for me, except kill roaches. That was my job. Her moment of capitulation allowed me to have her voice and image preserved when she died. Being able to see and hear her voice is a priceless gift and testament to choosing courage over hesitation or fear.

In 2015, I was accepted to the Master of Social Work Graduate Program at the University of Central Florida. I always wanted to be a therapist. Becoming a Licensed Clinical Social Worker was the means to this end. However, the timing was not right. Kids, jobs, and life interceded.

Six months after Yvette died, I reapplied and was again accepted. In August, I became a student/intern in the full-time program at UCF. I loved it! However, my body did not. I tried, despite knowing my fibromyalgia would probably make the task more challenging. I did it anyway. The school part was a piece of cake. The internship was another story. I was fortunate to be placed in a Title 9 elementary school and to work with a wonderful mentor named Sheila. I was at the school twice a week for 7 hours each day.

My experience of school social work was an education. Sheila was a work horse and we never stopped moving, being called into classrooms and dealing with crisis situations. Again, I loved it and felt like I finally knew what I wanted to be when I grew up. A therapist. Not a school social worker. That shit was hard, and I was no Sheila. The first year of the program was the generalist social work practicum and the second year would have been the clinical social work practicum. I never made it to the clinical promised land.

A week before the withdrawal without penalty period was over, I was dragging. I was emotionally, physically, and mentally exhausted. I was also pissed off that I was unable to handle the load physically. I was disappointed but made the decision to withdraw anyway. I would be lying if I said having to quit does not bother me still. What if? Why me? Insert pity party here.

The courage to follow through on going to graduate school after passing on it the first time was my victory, even though I never completed the program. I do not have to wonder what if any longer. It does not make my disappointment completely disappear, but it does mitigate it. Listening to my body and making the hard choice to withdraw did not render me a failure, even though it felt that way for many months. The decision to view the "failure" as an opportunity to practice self-care became my new reference point.

Courage

Courage does not always look like barging into a closed-door meeting to quit your job. Yvette did this once. She was mad as hell and not going to take it anymore. More often it is a quiet determination, sometimes accompanied by tears or stomach pains. The little gestures, thoughts, or movements can be the most powerful means of facing adversity or pain. The learning curve is generous when it comes to exercising bravery in our lives.

When bad things happen, we all want answers. Searching for a reason is a natural reaction as we attempt to make sense of what is happening. Good ole how and why, again. Personally, I have spent more time than I care to admit searching for a reason why I did not know I was gay until the age of 39. Even after writing my memoir *Switching Teams*, the question remained unanswered. I tried mightily to take to heart the advice and wisdom of those who insisted that "everything happens for a reason" when everything changed in my family's world.

The intent of offering solace by assigning the "happens for a reason" mindset falls short. It is the go-to response offered when we are at a loss for words or unable to improve a terrible situation. It is like telling someone who has just lost their sight to look on the bright side. The parents of a twenty-six-year-old woman I had known for years once told me she needed to undergo a mastectomy because of breast cancer. My heart broke. I felt sick and fought back tears. I wonder what their reaction would have been had I responded with "everything happens for a reason."

My only response was how sorry I was and what could I do to help them. Moments like this led me to the decision to remove the

Moving Through

canned response from my pantry. Most mean well and their intentions are to offer an encouraging reminder of the big picture and grand design of the universe, but is it really the best we have?

No one enjoys watching their friends, family, or anyone for that matter, experience change, disappointment, or tragedy. Sometimes words do not suffice. Not every situation is life or death, but it often feels that way for the person who is struggling. Trying to convince someone the answer and purpose of their pain will one day be revealed does little to lift their spirits in that dark moment.

Dark moments are called dark for a reason. There is little light that shines on a couple who is breaking up or divorcing, or on a child who is being bullied for being different, or on anyone facing any variety of challenging moments. The last thing my kids needed to hear the day I told them I was gay, or their second mother was going to die, was that everything happens for a reason.

Many deeply faithful people believe that everything happens for a reason, which is not in itself a bad thing. This deeply held belief helps them muster strength to move through the mud. However, even the most faithful have moments of doubt and anger when something unexpected or awful happens.

Reasons are unnecessary for understanding or coping with trying times. If not careful, we can spend a lifetime trying to figure out why things happen and miss what is right before our eyes. How we rally after the fact is more important than trying to figure out why something happened. For others, ask yourself what you would want to hear in your darkest times, and say that. Say nothing and hug them if they need it. Saying I am sorry you are in pain, suffering, or struggling right now is also an option. Cry with them. Offer to help by asking them what they need. If they say nothing, do nothing. Knowing that you are there for them will be enough.

For ourselves, accept that in every difficult situation there are countless opportunities for growth, learning, and bravery when the storm begins. Seek comfort before answers. Resist the urge to let the search for answers become the focus of the path forward. Trust that if a reason exists, it will eventually be revealed when it is time for the lesson.

Reflect on the times when you were feeling lost, upset, or just plain wrecked and choose empathy first. Next time someone you know is going through the ringer, be mindful of how you respond to them. It is possible to be courageous without knowing the answers.

I encourage you to be gentle with yourself and to review the inventory in your fortitude shop. If your stock is low, restock. Breathe and reach out for support if the journey feels overwhelming or lonely.

15 - FORGIVENESS

What does forgiveness have to do with making peace with the past or moving through? Everything. Dealing with baggage unearths roots which run deep. Feeling wronged and not knowing what to do about it is another block to authenticity. Living in a state of guardedness is not a healthy way to operate. Protecting ourselves is a defense mechanism and part of survival mode. When the threat is gone, what is left sticks to us unless we make a concerted effort to let go or better yet, let be.

Forgiveness is a daily part of my life. Making the decision to sign a DNR and end medical care still haunts me. Though the decision was the right one, there are days when the wind still gets knocked out of me. Letting go of the anger and disappointment with the health care team assembled during her last year of life is a work in progress. The comedy of errors surrounding Yvette's passing is beyond comprehension. Questioning what could have been done differently has waned over time but still creeps in. Trusting the diagnosis, opinions, and follow-up care did not end well.

Carrying around the anger and disbelief propelled me through a few especially difficult days. My motivation was justice. Forgiveness was the last thing on my mind. Forgiving the medical community for letting her fall through the cracks won't bring her back. Stripping away the emotions, I know that cancer caused her death. Not her inadequate medical care.

In the early days, I channeled my anger by flipping the bird as I drove by the oncology office in town. Avoidance also did little to quiet my anger. I tried valiantly for months to take routes which would not take me anywhere near the hospital. The visual reminders triggered me every time. It has taken months to fully accept that cancer does what it wants. And did so in grand dramatic fashion. Assigning blame is easy but ultimately blocked forward progress. What is done is done. No amount of anger, questioning, or disappointment changes that.

Letting go of the outcome and the path which led to the death of my wife had to become my goal. Forgiveness is letting go of the responsibility to carry anger. In addition to my anger with the healthcare community, I was harboring resentment and anger towards the people in her life who really did a number on her. Two months after she died, a private memorial was planned on the beach. The reservation was finalized months before she passed and was intended to be a social gathering for a married lesbian couple's retreat we'd organized. Keeping the reservation was difficult.

Instead of cancelling the hotel reservation, I went alone. My first solo weekend was an exercise in moving through, very ungracefully. The solitude was unsettling. For the first time in years, my beach buddy was not present. I missed her in my bones. Going anyway was my first step outside of my widow comfort zone. The first night I stayed in the room except for a brief trip out to grab a slice of pizza. I grabbed my backpack and walked three blocks. It felt like I scaled Everest. I had my backpack in one hand and the pizza box in the other. As I approached the parking garage I froze. With both hands full, I had no way to reach in the back pocket of the backpack to get the room key. Putting down the box on the ground seemed gross, so I pathetically asked an approaching older couple if they could reach in the open pocket and grab my key out of it.

In the past, she would have been the one with the key. My failsafe was gone. I thanked the couple and tears immediately followed. Night one was ugly. I never ate the pizza and spent a good hour sobbing on the phone with my breathe, focus, and be present friend Tony. My stalwart companion talked with me long enough for the anxiety medication to kick in and I went to bed. Sleeping alone at home was hard enough, being in the empty hotel room was suffocating. The darkness was overwhelming and the noise of the ocean off the balcony was anything but calming. Me, myself, and I were happy to watch the sun rise the next morning.

The next day, I received a text from her son asking me for some of her ashes. He and I had little to no communication after she died. I could not believe he would randomly reach out on the day of her private memorial on the beach. My immediate reaction was to tell him no. I was angry. Having ringside seats to the pain of their

Forgiveness

estrangement put me in the front row of the struggle bus. The late afternoon bonfire was hours away and I was now pissed off. Great.

After firing off some explicit texts to Blue, she gently reminded me that hanging on to the anger and resentment was not going to end well for me. The suggestion to consider forgiveness made me furious, however I knew it was exactly what I had to do. This was a big ask. I sat on a bench looking at the water and realized that Yvette was gone. Really gone. I had become so accustomed to fighting her battles alongside her. I was her support and hype man when things were blowing up. As much as I wish I could have been the voice of the high road to her, I just could not get there while she was alive. Watching a loved one suffer emotionally was not the time for practicing objectivity or forgiveness.

She was gone. I gave myself permission to let go of the responsibility of carrying the torch of anger toward those who caused her pain. It was no longer my job to fight her battles. She was gone. While relieved, the thought made me ugly cry for a long time.

Letting go of the resentment felt like letting go of a part of me, and worse yet, her. She was gone but releasing my anger did not mean I was letting go of her. I know she would have wanted me to stop the battle. She forgave the unforgivable her entire life, frequently at her own expense. My choice slowly nudged my journey of healing and set in motion my plan to make peace with her son and their past.

Moving Through

The bonfire was exactly as it should have been. Being surrounded by friends was the reward for the rough days leading up to my first solo adventure. Two days later, I invited her son over to give him some ashes. He arrived at the same house he wanted nothing to do with for the past seven years. My plan was to meet him at the door and hand him the ashes. He did not look at me when I opened the door. Instead of a give and go, I asked him to come inside and sit down. I needed to talk to him.

We sat facing one another on the couch and I handed him the silver box with her ashes in them. He opened it and smiled. I asked him if he wanted a collage of photos of himself and his mom which was on the wall. He did. As I handed him the collage, he looked up. Our eyes met and I got goosebumps. I had forgotten he had her eyes. Exactly. It was like I was looking at her. With that nudge, I told him I had a couple of things to say.

I told him I loved him but was angry with him for a long time. He apologized and took responsibility for his part. The rest of the conversation was sincere, heartfelt, and teary-eyed. It ended when I asked him to honor her by remembering to be more like her as he lived his life. She was the best person any of us had ever known. Letting go of the animosity and focusing on the present moment helped us both move beyond the past.

Forgiving someone else takes courage and a commitment to move beyond the past. Part of the struggle Yvette faced was blaming herself for the break down in the relationship with her son. If only she was a better mother, if only she did this, if only, if only, if only. She held herself responsible for every bad act simply because she raised him. She beat herself up for many years. Near the end of her life, she was finally able to understand she was not to blame for his reactions or behavior after she divorced. She did everything right, however the results did not show it. Instead of being angry with him, she blamed herself.

Stipulation. It is easier to forgive others than it is ourselves. We all have regrets and events which we can't help but beat ourselves up about. Playing these instances on a continual loop affects how we move through and interact with the world.

Learning to view ourselves through a kinder and more compassionate lens is another big ask for people who are resistant to viewing themselves in a positive light. Humans fail every day. We fail our families, partners, friends, and strangers. The accumulation of these failures throughout a lifetime becomes overwhelming and stunts the ability to move through and live the best life possible.

Judgement is the sister to self-loathing. Becoming friends with ourselves can break the hold of the inner critic and squash the tendency to judge the world harshly. It is challenging to forgive others when judgement colors the worldview. Those who are prone to judging others unfairly judge themselves the same way. Conflict within makes easing conflict with others, and forgiveness, an impossible task. Digging in and taking a stand keeps us stuck. It hardens us to the beauty around us and prevents love from taking its rightful place in life.

To forgive is not to say that what happened was acceptable. Forgiveness is a mindset as well as an action. It is the decision to no longer allow poison to contaminate our souls. The ability to forgive is inversely proportionate to the degree of wrong committed. Small transgressions are more easily forgiven. Contrition for our transgressions to others is within our control.

Saying I am sorry to someone does not erase or rewrite the past, but it does allow healing to begin. It is the starting point for the process of healing. In twelve-step programs, Step 8 is making a list of persons harmed and a willingness to make amends. Step 9 is the action of directing those amends to the person wronged. Step 8 is the mindset and Step 9 is the action part.

Being willing to make amends is hard, doing so is even harder. What happens when we feel wronged and no amends may be forthcoming? Forgiving those who lack any intention of making amends requires a new perspective.

Forgiveness is not about the other person. Read that again please. It is about freeing up energy within to move past pain or heartache. It is not a one and done proposition. Believing forgiveness is a free pass for bad behavior is toxic and inhibits growth. Forgive and forget is a lie. For some acts, forgiveness is impossible to imagine. I am sorry means an effort not to repeat the behavior is recognized.

Learning to accept apologies allows emotional and mental obstacles to clear out. Unspeakable acts are forgivable but not easily forgotten. So many struggle to forgive others but the true root of the problem lies within. Carrying around self-loathing is an indicator of a lack of forgiveness for ourselves. Bullies are a perfect example of what happens when internal chaos spills out into the world.

In elementary school my son experienced bullying. This was his first lesson in "hurt people, hurt people" class. Being teased for whatever reason made him feel awful and angry. Explaining the virtue in looking past the hurt was a hard sell for a six-year-old. My first instinct as a mother was to go full momma bear on this kid, who happened to live next door. I wanted to tell my son to punch him in the face but did not. Instead, I explained that bullies behaved that way because they did not have peace in their lives and needed to make other people feel small so they could feel better about themselves. He was not buying it. Truthfully, taking the high road is exhausting.

I pointed out a few concrete examples and tried to appeal to his sense of sympathy. This boy was struggling at home. His life was harder than any six-year-old should have to deal with. I looked past the behavior and focused on the why. Teaching my son to look at the big picture was my goal. There is always something behind the scenes happening which we may not be privy to. Allowing this bully to affect how my son saw himself was not acceptable. The behavior sucked but creating an awareness of what might be going on which fueled his actions allowed my son to let the words roll down his back.

Forgiving someone who lacks contrition, awareness, or acceptance of their part is like running face first into a brick wall. The impact stings, but the resulting scrapes, bruises, or broken noses heal

Moving Through

eventually. Religions teach forgiveness in absolute terms. A priest once told me that forgiveness is not about accepting the unacceptable moving forward. Fool me once, shame on me. Fool me twice, shame on you thinking. Moving through the maze of forgiveness is not going back for more. Carrying around anger, hurt, and hostility chips away at our spirit. Over time, the spirit begins to collapse on itself and peace is crushed. Learning to step away from those who continually behave unkindly or angrily is needed to facilitate healing a broken spirit.

Focusing on the emotions attached helps activate the journey of forgiveness. Acknowledging mistakes made from an objective viewpoint is step one in untethering the grip. Viewing shortcomings as opportunities to learn taps the wheel along. Developing an awareness of the inner critic popping up follows. Asking others for input puts things in perspective when inundated with the nagging negative inner voices.

Finding it in your heart to forgive yourself and release the pressure valve is a necessity. The starting point is making the decision to let yourself off the hook. How we speak to ourselves must be as kind as most are to their loved ones. The horrible person tape must be destroyed. Tossed out. Set ablaze. While watching the bonfire burn, begin replacing the negative self-talk with one positive thought. Interrupting the loop is a choice, takes practice, and often requires professional help. Being open to the process of changing the dialogue in your head is one small step forward.

Some mistakes can be fixed, but others cannot. Gaining clarity will help determine the wrongs which can be righted. Interpreting the gravity of an offense is subjective and our own perspective cannot always be trusted. People are notorious for being their own worst critics and better at giving advice than taking it. Flipping the script means asking yourself what you would say to a friend in the same situation. Would you tell a friend they were horrible? How about beyond redemption? Didn't think so.

Surrendering to the process puts the brain on notice and allows the heart to entertain the idea of letting go and letting be. When the heart and brain are on the same page our behavior follows suit. The programming changes when our inner dialogue changes. As we think so shall we be.

The most pervasive demons are born in our own minds and enjoy fabricating untruths about who we are. Creating new rules for living begins with loving who we are and ending the search for perfection. The authentic self cannot flourish if the demons are running the factory. Flawed people are everywhere. As in, every single person on earth. Without forgiveness, the ability to be and love who we are ourselves is compromised.

When in doubt, choose forgiveness even if it seems counterintuitive. Letting go will let light in, remove the blocks to forward progress, and free up space for healthy relationships to become the rule rather than the exception.

16 - RELATIONSHIPS

Forging healthy relationships is the holy grail of adulting. The relationships we enter shine a light on our internal dialogue. Whether at home or at the workplace, who we associate with can impact how we see ourselves. The state of our relationships is a good indicator of our internal wellness. Learning to interpret relationships through an objective lens gives a more accurate picture of what is happening beneath the surface.

Putting health and wellness above all else is not popular when toxic relationships or difficult people are involved. Dealing with baggage, chaos, fear, regret, and the many roadblocks to authenticity may be the beginning of the journey but learning to engage in healthy interactions with others is the litmus test of progress toward peace.

A healthy relationship has healthy boundaries. What does this look like? The power of healthy boundaries requires an understanding of how to express acceptable behavior to people. Asserting a boundary without feeling guilt, shame, or fear is difficult when dealing with established patterns of past behavior. We teach people how to treat us and changing up the dance is not often met with applause.

Family, friends, or acquaintances who are accustomed to being one way do not take kindly to changes in the rules of acceptable behavior. We are all familiar with physical boundaries. Respecting personal space and maintaining the invisible area directly near our bodies. If you have ever been to a theme park, you know what not respecting personal space looks and feels like.

Boundary setting is a complicated concept, especially for those who may not be used to expressing themselves in a healthy way. Many struggle to let others know how they are really feeling or what they need from them. The reasons are varied and often based in fear.

Fear is the other F word. People who are afraid of disappointing, upsetting, or rejecting others often have the hardest time setting healthy boundaries. We are all entitled to decide for ourselves what we want, need, and expect out of the relationships we choose to be a part of.

After I came out, my boundaries were tested daily. In the chaos, I forgot that I could keep them intact as I tried to make other people feel better about what was happening. Becoming confident with ourselves and in tune with our own needs is the first step in creating healthy boundaries. See where I am going here? The success of boundary setting means taking a close look at what is going on inside of us on the front end.

Moving Through

Relationships are difficult enough when good boundaries are in place. We all bring varying degrees of baggage to whatever relationship we may find ourselves in. Family, friends, work, or romantic relationships do not exist in a vacuum. Our interconnectedness is unavoidable unless you choose to live on the side of a mountain in Asia.

Arriving at the place where we know who we are and what our boundaries are is only half of the battle. This does not guarantee success in the boundary setting department when it comes to enforcement of those boundaries with others.

Here is where it can be tricky. Respecting our own boundaries, once we decide what they may be, is easy. However, what are we supposed to do when others refuse to comply? Not so easy. Setting boundaries does not guarantee compliance on the other end.

There are plenty of boundary resistors in the world. I bet we all can name a few right off the top of our heads. These are the people who, despite our best attempts to make clear the rules, have no problem ignoring them. When you encounter someone who falls in this category it can be challenging to maintain your ground and not be tempted to relax the rules out of a sense of keeping the peace.

What about family boundaries? What happens when setting healthy boundaries creates tension or estrangement? Setting boundaries is something we do for ourselves. Not everyone will accept a boundary. Drawing a line in the sand does not ruin relationships. Reactions do. What if someone reacts negatively? What if they are angry? In my experience, they will either get over it or they won't. Either way you are choosing you, which is a win. Feeling responsible for keeping someone else's peace, while sacrificing your own, is an exercise in futility.

Fight the urge to allow what is unacceptable for yourself in order to not make waves or rock the boat. No one wins in this scenario. The peace that ends up being lost is your own. Unfortunately, some are not equipped with the tools necessary to comply.

Be warned. Boundary smashers are everywhere and come in all shapes and sizes. Continually being in a situation where boundaries are ignored or argued is not acceptable. Brace yourself for what I am about to say next. It is perfectly acceptable to let go of anyone who is a slow learner or dead set on challenging your boundaries. Without explanation or argument. Period.

Is this unfortunate? Yes. Does this make you a horrible person? No. The beauty in life lies in the fact that we are all worthy of deciding who we want in our lives. Sometimes you must make hard choices for the sake of your own peace. With practice, it will become much easier to detect and deal with those who have a hard time taking no for an answer.

Working to limit instances when things go sideways is not an easy task, but when we handle our own shit our chance of success is greater. When we manage ourselves, we are in the unique position of teaching others the value and benefit of boundaries.

Knowing our own boundaries acts as the foundation. The sturdiness of our relationship house depends upon pouring the slab thoughtfully and carefully. We cannot control who comes and knocks at the door, but we can determine when someone will be allowed through it.

Take time each day to review your own boundaries. Pay close attention to the boundaries set by others and respect them just as you would want yours to be respected. Mutual understanding goes a long way toward creating relationships that have substance and longevity. Rest assured that setting healthy boundaries is one way we can improve ourselves and make our relationships stronger and healthier.

As part of her healing process, Yvette created a video four months before she died. She spoke about life after a toxic relationship. Her words are powerful and encouraging.

"In a relationship there are two people. For that relationship to be healthy both people have to be healthy. In order to do that you have to take a long hard look at yourself and address issues and traumas that happened in your life. There is no way around it. Believe me. I have tried every which way but directly to it. If you don't address it, it's just going to manifest itself and create unnecessary issues in your life. In the end, you are going to waste a lot of time and many years being unhappy when there is no reason for it.

I had a 22-year marriage, 24 years total, with a very toxic person. By the time I got through that, there was some damage that was done. In fact, the last three months of that marriage, from the time I came out to the time I moved out was probably one of the most traumatic periods of my life. So, I thought, okay, I'm out, I'm proud, I'm gay, I'm free. Yay! Everything is going to be great. I am in love and Dawn and I move in together and we start our life together and I don't think about my ex

Relationships

anymore. I'm done. Once that divorce was finalized, I put him and 24 years in a box, put it on the shelf, and not dealing with that anymore because I made it out.

The truth of the matter is I didn't make it out because the stink came out of the box and came into the life I was trying to create with my wife. Old messages, old habits, old trauma. Everything seeped through because I refused to deal with what happened. Not talking about it does not help it go away. Being open, honest, and authentic is where you start, and this is where I am starting.

I spent the last few years in therapy. I've dealt with my childhood and the abuse from my childhood and skipped right over my marriage. I thought, "Well I did all the work in my childhood I should be good. Why are all these things popping up? Why do I keep having these reactions? What does this trigger me? What's going on? Why can't I find that real true happiness that I long for? I mean I have a good life, I have a great wife, we have great kids, we get to do our own thing and run our businesses. What do I still feel this underlying misery?

It's basically because in the 22-year long marriage to this very toxic, I now understand narcissist, I was told over and over and over again what a horrible person I was. I did everything wrong. Everything was my fault. It was unbelievable I had that kind of power. And yet felt so helpless. The beauty of narcissists is they turn it around and make you feel like you did it, they are the victim, they have no power, they have no voice, and poor me. All the meanwhile they are running a scam on you. It took me 6 years after coming out and leaving the marriage to fully understand the effect that person had on me and what I needed to do to be healthy.

Moving Through

The message basically is, Dawn's favorite expression "handle your shit." You have to handle your shit. You do not leave bad relationships without some stuff on you. It is important to get help and important for you to talk about and not ignore it. Ignoring it does not make the problem go away.

I was married to a man who made it his mission to control everything about our lives and me. I am not very easily controlled so I feel really stupid sitting here talking to you about coming out of a 22-year marriage being controlled and not even really understanding what was happening because I fought back. When I got angry enough and started cursing, or even throwing a chair across the room, then it was my fault that the whole thing happened. Time and again everything was my fault and I was reminded I was a bad mother, horrible spouse, and unsympathetic person.

One of the things he said to me right before I left the house was "your girlfriend is going to dump your ass when she finds out what a bitch you are." Really? And you know the most messed up part of that was I believed him. I believed him. So, I go off on this new life and I carry that with me. And every step of the way I am waiting for my girlfriend, now wife, to dump me because she is going to find out what a horrible bitch I am and in fact everything that is wrong in the world and in her life is my fault. This is the kind of thing narcissists do to you.

Find the resources. They are out there and don't keep things quiet. That was part of the problem I had. I didn't tell anybody for 22 years what was going on in my house. At all. I felt so ashamed by what was happening and so stupid, and so beaten down I kind of thought everything was my

Relationships

fault after a while. I just never said anything to anybody and that is the biggest problem.

If you are stuck in a situation, speak up. Go to your friends, go to your family, there are resources out there. Get out of the relationship. It's bullshit and it is never going to get better. I always tried to be the best wife I could and maybe if I did this and maybe if I tried that and maybe if I gave in to this it would get better. Suck it up. You made this vow. You have to stay. You made this bed and you have to lie in it. It never got any better, in fact it got worse.

The older he got, the worse he got. Finally, in the very end I was like fuck this bullshit and I had to leave. Unfortunately, I packed some of the bullshit with me and that is the point of my video today. You never leave a toxic situation without something stuck to you. If you really want to be healthy and have a healthy relationship and be authentic and feel free you need to get the help that is out there. You need to get help for yourself.

Seek out your therapist. There are really good ones out there and begin rebuilding your self-esteem, your self-confidence, and rewiring the voice in your head telling you you're no good or the cause of every problem that ever happens or whatever other crap that got stuck in your head says. I know I have a pile of it in mine.

It's okay to have a trauma that fucks you up. I don't think most people want to admit that. I don't think most people know that it is okay. It is okay. What's not okay is not addressing it, not looking at it, and not trying to move through it so you can be happy and feel free. Look, I know it is scary. I am doing it. I am doing it with sweating palms and a racing heart. Trust the process. Trust yourself. All those things that you were told were lies. They were not true. You are valuable, and you are loved, and you are worth it. You need to choose you and stop listening to the voices in your head that create chaos and confusion. You can do it."

17 - THE BLAME GAME

Ever had those days when everyone and everything is annoying? Here is a tip I learned a long time ago from a wise woman. If everything is bothering you, it cannot be everyone. It's you. The quintessential example and proof that sometimes it is me and not you. When relationships become strained there is a tendency to blame the other person for the tension.

Relationships at their end can be subtle, follow a natural progression, and end peacefully. Others end in a blaze of anger, resentment, and pain. Most fall somewhere in the middle. In a perfect world, the first reaction should be to make a serious attempt to communicate feelings in a rational and kind way. In the real world, many of us are just not there yet. We have not quite perfected the act of detaching from our emotions in order to tackle our conflicts from a purely rational and calm state. It takes time and a true understanding of what our part in the situation may be. And sometimes reading a helpful pin about healthy relationships on Pinterest.

Moving Through

It is natural to feel afraid when a relationship ends. When a marriage ends, everything changes. Entering the dating world is not something most look forward to. The process of learning about a new person is scary enough. New beginnings bring their own special version of fear to the party.

With any luck, we have taken notes and learned something about ourselves which helps create relationships that are healthy in the future. Part of the process is to focus on trying to understand why a relationship ended rather than considering what we need to do moving forward. There are many reasons why relationships end. However, what trips us up moving forward often has nothing to do with what happened.

The only way to truly assess what the issue may be is by being honest. First with ourselves and then with the other person. We are human and unfortunately prone to misunderstanding, operating with expectations, and holding unspoken resentment with those in our lives who we care about the most. Honesty may not solve the issue at hand, but it will bring to the surface the real problem and clarity about whether moving forward is possible.

The ability to thoughtfully communicate needs and feelings can be compromised if you are a product of an unhealthy environment. My ex-husband and I were facilitators for wedding prep at our church. Our session centered on communication. The feelings wheel was our reference point. Google what one looks like if you have no clue what I am talking about. Along with this tool was a worksheet which explained how using "I" statements when communicating could diffuse conflict and help the other person hear how the speaker was feeling. Mandatory lessons in how to implement "I" statements for everyone in the world would change the face of our planet.

So, what exactly am I talking about? An "I" message shifts the focus to the feelings, or thoughts and beliefs, of the speaker instead of assigning them to the listener. "I" statements neutralize the blame game. For example, a person might say to his or her partner, "I feel worried and abandoned when you stay out late with your friends without texting or calling to let me know you are going to be late" instead of demanding, "Why are you never home on time?"

"I" statements perfectly illustrate why catching flies with honey is preferred to vinegar. Learning to identify how we are feeling below the surface helps foster awareness and kindness in our interactions. Becoming an expert in recognizing how to properly assess our own emotions is up to each of us. It does take practice and is not always an automatic response in the beginning.

Becoming adept at labeling emotions is the first step. If we cannot identify how, or what, we are feeling, it is unfair to expect others to be able to help us by reading our minds. Survival mode stifles emotions. If you have been in survival mode for any reason you may need to consult with a professional to learn how to navigate emotions in a healthy way. It is unreasonable to believe that healthy communication can exist in a volatile and finger pointing environment.

As much as we joked about the feeling wheel at the time, it really did work. The skills we learned by teaching others came in handy when my husband and I eventually divorced. The first time Yvette and I had a couple's discussion, meaning argument, she was surprised to learn there was a way to disagree without name calling or blaming each other. It was what she was used to in her first marriage. Being blamed for every problem that happened over a twenty-four-year time span was her normal. She was always ready for a conflict and a screaming match.

Engaging in "I" statements with her was a foreign concept and took time for her to get used to. Retooling the approach to conflict has also been an adjustment for my new wife. She too became conditioned to being blamed by her ex for everything that was wrong in their marriage. She was even blamed for her ex's infidelity. Nice. Despite knowing the reality, being told something repeatedly creates self-doubt and people begin to believe it as the truth.

It is easy to blame someone else for a breakdown in a relationship. We are all guilty of this. It is important to keep in mind the baggage, opinions, perceptions, and experiences being brought to the dining table. Being able to understand ourselves prior to sitting down is a prerequisite for the dinner. Understanding that dessert may include a heaping plate of letting go is the hardest part. Some people are just jerks. Sounds harsh, but it is true. Often people struggle to get out of their own way and expect others to forsake their own needs in order to control the outcome. Not cool.

The ability to get past our own negative feelings is an important step in the effort to mend a relationship. It may not always be enough to overcome a challenge or change a situation, but in the end will go a long way in freeing up valuable mental and emotional real estate within. Every relationship is unique and learning to let go of those that were only for a season or are no longer healthy is not easy. Ripping off the Band-aid does not always offer a quick resolution. Unfortunately, some operate with a selfish need to keep reinjuring the site when things are not moving in their desired direction. This is never acceptable.

Interestingly, many commented they did not realize how hard my divorce and coming out process was because they could not tell from looking at me. Was I supposed to fall apart? Everyone else was falling apart. Someone had to keep it together and steer the damaged boat. The reality; I was wrecked in every way imaginable. I was responsible for the wreckage, was a first responder to the aftermath, and was surrounded by sadness and pain that took years to subside.

The pain of losing my marriage to my husband of 20 years did not slide off me. It stuck like pollen to lawn furniture in spring. I carried it inside and waited for my time to fall apart. There never seemed to be a good or convenient time for a breakdown. I had one good semi-breakdown the day I signed my divorce papers. I curled up in a ball and laid in my youngest son's bed for hours. Other than that, nothing. I put one foot in front of the other and kept moving forward while carefully making sure everyone else's wounds were healing properly after the wreck.

I will share my secret. I was in survival mode. In the quiet moments alone, my superhero cape helped soak up the tears, absorbed the pain, and was my blanket while I endured absolute heartbreak. My takeaway has been to be more open and honest when I am asked the hard questions. I have also let go of feeling alienated by those who acted on the assumption that I happily breezed through this challenging time.

In the eyes of many, the only reason I got divorced was because "I turned lesbian." This is a hard one for me. While it's an obvious conclusion, it does not entirely represent the scope of the circumstances. Of course, it was the precipitating factor in my leaving, but there were other issues between my ex and I that were less apparent to the outside world. Explaining these issues on the back end has been frustrating because the gay umbrella covered the rain which puddled beneath our relationship for years.

The issues we had were not blatantly obvious to anyone other than ourselves. We worked privately to address the areas we struggled with. Airing our marital laundry was never how we rolled. Only a select few, in my very small inner circle, knew of the struggles. Everyone else's opinion of our relationship was based on what they saw on the surface. Of course they did not know that my marriage was not perfect, it was not their place to know.

The truth was, we were much better friends than spouses to one another. We were different people in many ways, but we cared deeply for one another and tried our best to mitigate the differences as we began a family and created a life together for almost 20 years.

We communicated differently and our understanding of how to meet each other's needs on an emotional level was an obstacle we could never quite conquer. The truth is, our marriage was not going to withstand the test of time. When we were able to verbalize and accept the truth, we began our healing. Reaching this place of agreement made the divorce real and was an acknowledgment that our challenges predated my delayed awareness of my sexual orientation.

If I had a dollar for every time I heard "I did not know that" when asked about my first marriage I would be writing in Belize from my yacht. In hindsight, I do not regret keeping our issues private.

Assigning blame for outcomes is a natural reaction when things do not go as planned. We all do it. Having the ability to evaluate ourselves and our part in situations is a skill learned over time. Who wants to admit to their own shortcomings and how they may have played a part in how it all went down? He never blamed me for being gay or for why our marriage eventually failed. I never blamed him either. We both learned how to be better spouses to our current spouses because of what we faced together.

Remember that figuring out fault is best saved for insurance adjusters or ambulance chasing attorneys. Florida is a no-fault state for divorce, but that is a legal term and does not stop people from searching for a target to direct the blame toward. In my situation, gay became the perfect scapegoat.

Learning to resist the urge to make assumptions and jump to conclusions based on pieces of a story is not easy, but it's an important part of supporting each other. As tempting as it may be to blame someone else for a breakdown in a relationship or outcome of an event, carefully considering our own role should be the first step in the process. Accepting responsibility for our part is how we learn to move forward and feel peace in the future.

While some may never understand the intricacies of my journey or completely accept the path my life has taken, correcting inaccurate assumptions is an opportunity to help create a better understanding of each other and our stories. Our shoe sizes or styles vary but if we choose to look at the wear marks on the soles instead of the pretty boxes sitting on the shelf, understanding is possible. Being negative takes zero energy. Learning to shift thinking requires self-awareness and self-control, and these two skills are always within our control. Bummer, I know. Eliminating moments of negative thinking is not the goal. Learning how to avoid becoming stuck is the goal. Stuck is no way to live a peace filled life.

What does unstuck look like and what steps are recommended for someone who is struggling with feeling stuck? The first tool out of the box is about letting go of the past. What's done is done. Limping along serves no one. Accepting when things work out as we hoped just as happily as when they do not is step three. What medium are you using to create your canvas? Fear? Negativity? Apathy?

Finding the value in reflecting upon the events of our lives in order to learn, grow, and move toward healing is not possible without letting go. Processing the events in life is part of the journey. Although unpleasant, it is the key to moving forward. Coming to terms with the idea that life will always include challenges, trials, and tribulations is another helpful tip. No one is immune from

The Blame Game

difficulty, but we can immunize ourselves if we understand the role fear plays in remaining stuck.

When we rise above fear and uncertainty, we grow in ways we never imagined. It is possible to learn just as much from relationships which have ended as those which remain. Choosing an honest, humble, and fearless approach is necessary in order to have peace. Creating healthy boundaries with people in our lives is a key part of the equation.

Fear is often the reason some accept the unacceptable for the sake of maintaining a relationship which may be on its last legs. It is often easier to remain in a relationship that is unhealthy rather than risk being alone. Trusting our instincts when it comes to making decisions about where people fit in life is the starting point. Our gut never lies. Fear of change is the driving force for many who find themselves in unhealthy relationships. The devil you know is better than the devil you don't. Choosing yourself above all else applies even in relationships.

18 - BE YOURSELF

The first step in being yourself is to figure out who you are. So, I must ask, who are you? If your mind went blank and jaw dropped, you are not alone. Many struggle with or spend little time searching for an answer.

Before someone can be who they are, they first need to understand and know who they are. Lurking within the "be yourself" movement is a mindset that information is power and an honest search for the truth will magically guarantee happiness and peace in life. Just be yourself. What does that mean? How does someone achieve the goal?

Knowing who you are is a lifelong process which requires the ability to discern the difference between being and doing. Understanding the core of our being is the goal. We are trained at an early age to seek approval from those closest to us. When this approval is missing, we begin to believe we are not good enough.

Often people respond to the question by listing what they do. Asking someone to describe themselves is one way to discover who they believe themselves to be. The answer may or may not be accurate. When asked this question, I like to have fun with it. My reply is often to flip the script and ask who they think I am and is usually met with a sideways look.

The perception of self depends on who we think we are. Depending on the day, our beliefs can shift. There are core elements of who we are which stay consistent throughout life. Likes, dislikes, mannerisms, habits, and physical traits appear on this list.

Life events can stunt, damage, or impact the speed and ease in which self-discovery takes place. Expressing the truth of who we are can become challenging when the past has been hard. Even if we know the truth, the ability to express who we are and be ourselves unapologetically can be compromised and stifled when external pressure squeezes our internal selves to the point of suffocation.

Who we are at our core includes every facet of being. The good, bad, and ugly. There is a strong tendency to define who we are by how we look or act. Most people upon meeting will ask specific questions about what they do for a living.

In order to answer the question of who we are, we must examine the elements that interrupt our ability to live authentically. My son is in the process of training to become an electrician. As a result, I have become interested in how electricity is created and behaves. Comparing the road to authenticity and the behavior of electrical circuits shows many parallels.

A crash course in physics may help connect the dots. Electricity is the flow of electrical power, or charge. Every human being alive is an energy source. The flow of energy depends on many factors. Electric current is defined as the rate at which charge flows through a surface, usually a wire. Life energy, or current, flows out through our bodies, minds, and souls. The motion of our lives also creates a current of energy.

How easily the current flows along a path, life or electrical, depends on the environment and structure of the circuit. If you are an exercise enthusiast, you know watts are one way the amount of energy expended during exercise can be measured. Also worth noting is the concept of impedance, which is exactly what it sounds like. Electrical impedance is the measure of the opposition a circuit presents to a current when a voltage is applied.

The magnitude of the current flowing in a path depends on the path's voltage and impedance. In other words, there are a slew of variables which can interrupt the flow of energy and create obstacles in the ability to be yourself and live authentically. Making the decision to be yourself and arriving at a place of certainty about who you are frequently upsets the apple carts of those around you. Internal certainty is not always appreciated or met with enthusiasm by those who are not secure in themselves or who are uncomfortable with change. The extent of the reactions depends on the degree of dysfunction present.

In unhealthy environments, survival hinges on learning to work around the resistance present and sacrificing ourselves for others for the sake of peace. Self-preservation is an authenticity killer.

Be Yourself

Fortunately, the idea that electricity, or our lives, only take the path of least resistance is a myth. Contrary to popular belief, electricity takes all paths available.

Now for the good news. Within each person lies the capacity to replace the ancient electrical panel and upgrade the wiring to remove anything impeding our journey. Overcoming and making peace with the past rewires our circuits. Being conditioned to go with the flow and conform begins at an early age. As time goes by our flow of energy is slowed, blocked, or clogged by circumstances outside our control. Who we are and the things we do are not the same thing. Who someone believes they are is subjective. Our self-image is a mashup of the two. The things we do can be a manifestation of who we are, but often who we are takes a subordinate position to the other.

Both are influenced by mindset, the past, and the specifics of an individual's life circumstances. Who you are is your purest state of being and what you do is action. If you are a doctor, you treat patients. Our "who" and our "do" often behave like Cain and Abel. The internal conflict creates external chaos, sends an inaccurate message, and creates unrealistic expectations about how we are supposed to live and behave. Who we are, and who we think we are, are not always perfectly aligned. The mind, body, and spirit all factor in when answering this question. Defining ourselves only by our daily activities, roles, and responsibilities is an easy trap to fall in to.

Discovering our true authentic self can be time consuming and emotionally, mentally, and physically exhausting. The search requires an investment of precious time, energy, and attention to the deepest parts of our being. Finding your true self is nothing like locating a lost set of keys.

"There is nothing rarer, nor more beautiful, than a woman being unapologetically herself; comfortable in her perfect imperfection. To me, that is the true essence of beauty." Maraboli, S. (2013)

Authenticity, change, and loving yourself go hand in hand. Changes related to how we think, or feel, are not always accompanied by physical or visible cues. Physical appearance is an obvious indicator of change but how do we measure what happens on the inside?

Eight years ago, I came out as a lesbian. Three years ago, I cut my hair short. It took months to renovate my wardrobe. My first suit was the cherry on the sundae of embracing my who. This simple act helped me realize that freedom and peace are byproducts of being comfortable in your own skin.

Confession time. As a stereotypical tomboy I never liked wearing dresses and remember being jealous of boys who got to wear suits to formal events. Shocker, right? Dressing for formal events has been a constant source of frustration and figuring out what to wear has been mentally and emotionally exhausting. For years the search focused on finding clothes which fit, looked good, and more importantly, made me feel good. I believed if I looked good that feeling good would happen automatically.

Here is the truth. Working from the outside in was how I thought change would happen. It took multiple attempts for me to find my sweet spot. My approach to win the war against my closet and to make peace with my appearance was flawed and many articles of clothing were sacrificed along the way. I would shop for things I thought I should wear. Most of those purchases ended up in the donation bin.

The hesitation to express my true self was rooted in the fear of being labeled, misunderstood, and judged as different. Sound familiar? Before coming out, I had a fear of people thinking I was gay. Yeah. That is hilarious, huh? Coming out was just the opening act of my show and not the grand finale.

The decades long battle with my wardrobe had nothing to do with the fabric, cut, or style of the clothes I put on my body. The problem was how I felt on the inside. Ring any bells? The turning point in the war happened when I began to understand how fear affected my thinking and impacted my self-confidence. Again, the bastard called fear tried to call the shots.

Although it is uncomfortable to look at photos of myself and see the transformation documented over time, it helped me respect and understand the process. I wondered how it was possible to not actually be authentic when at the time the photo was taken I thought I was being authentic. I also wondered what readers of *Switching Teams* would think if they discovered I was still a work in progress and wrestling with taking my own advice.

I even asked my late wife if I was being phony for all those years. She pointed out the act of taking pictures was how I was working things out. She saw it before I did. Change takes time and often includes a series of baby steps within giant leaps.

Buying a men's suit was just one of many encores in the concert of my life. This suit was just another outward expression of my inner journey which took years to complete. As certain as I was about my desire to buy a suit, I still had to fight thoughts of getting a grey or black one instead. My wife gently encouraged me "to not chicken out" and I listened.

The fit was amazing, literally and figuratively. Finally. To some it may just be a piece of clothing, but it was much more and my final stand against giving a flying fuck about what anyone else thinks.

The daily choice to be and love yourself is not always popular. Remember, opinions, doctrine, and beliefs are all obstacles to being authentic. It is easy to shrink down and become invisible when negativity and hate is blocking the path forward. Deferring to the easy is also oppressive and suffocating.

The decision to publicly share my journey was risky and outside the boundaries of my introvert comfort zone. Honestly, there have been days when hiding and quietly erasing my story from the world sounded enticing, however I would have robbed myself of growth. Instead I chose to follow Eleanor Roosevelt's advice to do one thing that scares you every day.

Explaining to someone how it is possible to dress in men's clothes and not want to be a man was a frequent activity. Answering questions about how I label myself is also common. I preferred to

Be Yourself

be labeled as Dawn Elizabeth Waters. Keep in mind, living authentically requires no explanation.

Unfortunately, those who struggle to have authenticity in their own lives often make it difficult for those who exist outside of the traditional mold society has deemed acceptable. Unique is not the new black yet, but progress is being made to change this.

Language is a funny thing, especially from small kids. One of my favorite kid-butchered sentences in my house was "I wanna stand." We were not talking about walking or standing up. Hearing this meant they understood what I was saying. I think of this sentence often, especially since I published *Switching Teams*. Numerous people reached out to me through email and private message with genuine questions about my journey. I did my best to answer honestly and with kindness. I responded without getting defensive or argumentative.

Those that were looking for a fight did find one from me. There have been countless comments posted on my social media that have been uplifting and full of gratitude and validation for my decision to write it.

There have also been a few naysayers pop up here and there. I expected it. Yesterday, a lifelong lesbian let me know it was "kinda boring" and she "could barely get through it." This comment might have brought my writing house of cards crashing down if I had thinner skin. Honestly, the book was not for everyone. No book is. There will always be those who may not relate to or feel a connection with my story, especially those who have only known being gay their entire lives.

The topic of coming out later in life was merely the vehicle that I chose to talk about the common things we experience in our lives, regardless of our sexual orientation, race, religious affiliation, or gender.

My intent was to offer a glimpse of my experience, but more importantly to paint a picture of how change affects each of our lives. Far and away, "how I could not have known that I was gay until after 17 years of marriage and only having experiences with men" is the most asked question. My response is the same each time. I don't know. This confounds me just as much as the next guy and I still have moments when I do not understand how I did not know this about myself. Trust me on this one.

I spent a long time beating myself up for what I did not know. But eventually, I had to put down the bat. When I did know, I acted on it. Reaching deep within to acknowledge this truth was difficult and frightening. These exchanges, with both my gay and straight brothers and sisters, all led me to a similar conclusion. People are not interested in moving past what does not make sense. In a perfect world, our goal is to strive to understand one another. However, finding the ability to move beyond or make sense of what we personally do not know is difficult.

I also can appreciate why when some know, they do not take immediate action. This is a hard pill to swallow, especially when life as you know it suddenly changes. We each have our own timeline and unique journey. Our stories, actions, and decisions should not be undermined by others' opinions or gaps in how our personal situation is processed by an outsider.

Our operating mindset is cultivated from our own experience and perception of the world. Every individual has their own story, complete with characters and plot lines which may not always follow reason, logic, or commonly accepted practices. Our lives are not meant to be carbon copies of one another. How boring would that be? It is within the differences that the potential for growth and acceptance is found.

Why does a lack of understanding prevent some from accepting a person when their personal story differs from their own? Why is it so important to grasp the how or why before we can fully accept the what? When did it become so difficult to embrace people that have dissimilar experiences from our own?

Dismissing the experiences which deviate from our own is dangerous. It is human nature to gravitate towards those with similar experiences, interests, and journeys. Our inability to accept and understand what we have not personally experienced creates unnecessary obstacles in all relationships. If we are not careful, our world will eventually shrink to the point of isolation.

By focusing on differences, we are more likely to ignore and forget the existence of the common threads woven throughout our varied plots and chapters. Our shared fabric includes the threads of love, compassion, peace, sadness, and even fear. Getting bogged down in the details of another's journey distracts us from achieving peace in our personal lives and the larger universe. Kindness is abandoned when we allow differences to erode our interest in one another as humans. The ultimate act of kindness is the ability to say "I do not understand" to someone without reacting harshly or passing judgement.

A lack of understanding is not an open invitation to criticize nor is it a license to judge. Dismissing those we do not understand is a pervasive form of judgement leading to reactions that erode our ability to relate to each other wholly. Pick a topic. Politics. Religion. Sports. For example, I do not understand why people collect memorabilia from Disney. I know many who fall under this category. Lovely people, really. My understanding of why they do what they do or how they came to know they were collectors is not required in order to interact or have a relationship with them.

There is plenty I do not understand. About people, about life, and especially about myself. Choosing to look beyond the why, or how, and see everyone as the beautifully flawed and infinitely capable creatures we are helps me be myself. Some days, I am more successful than others in achieving this goal. If you have kids you do this a million times a day, especially those with teenagers. While I may not understand something about someone else, I take comfort in the realization that it is not my job to procure the answers to anyone else's life other than my own. It is my job to be kind, even if I have not personally experienced the same thing.

One day I hope to have a better answer for those who inquire about my lesbian awareness timeline. Until then, my focus remains on the benefits of connecting with those who have shared experiences, while remembering there is more to learn from those who have experienced things I haven't or those that think, live, or exist differently than I do.

Transformation begins once we embrace authenticity and replace fear with self-acceptance and confidence. Self-love begins here. The timeline and methods may vary but must begin with a decision to live life according to your own terms. Being yourself is a one-man job. No one can decide who you are but yourself. Stripping away the labels is an internal process.

The world may think it knows who we are, but the power to be ourselves comes from within. No opinion, person, or institution has the power to determine who we are. Claiming our identity and discovering who we are opens the door to loving who you are.

19 - LOVE YOURSELF

Loving yourself. My favorite subject. I harp on it constantly because it is important. Most of the hiccups we experience can be traced back to difficulties with understanding and implementing a healthy relationship with ourselves.

In order to work toward and feel peace, you must know your value and worth separate from any person, place, or thing. It is virtually impossible to live authentically if you do not like yourself. Liking, and loving, who you are is a critical piece in the puzzle. Is the voice in your head offering more cheers or jeers daily? Many are under the delusion that for self-acceptance and self-love to happen you must be perfect in every way. Not true. Loving who you are means loving all of you, even the dark parts.

My obsession with this concept exists because without this ingredient, the cake will not rise. Yes, I am comparing a peace filled life to baking a cake. I still receive messages from *Switching Teams* readers who are in various stages of the coming out, after having been married, process. A common theme found within these messages is self-doubt, self-criticism, and guilt. I understand the battle. Guilt is a love disruptor. In order to practice self-love, mindfulness is required. Loving ourselves provides a shield against the flying piles of garbage that the world can toss at us on any given day. We all have buttons that, when pushed, can make us question our greatness. In simple terms, the energy we put out into the world passes through the filter of how we feel about ourselves. Examining the source of the filter is work and often painful. Do it anyway. It is impossible to love yourself if you continue to hate the journey which brought you there.

We all experience "one of those days" moments. The days where nothing seems to go as planned, anything we touch crumbles into a mess right before our eyes, or we just feel lousy. Is this bad luck? Or is it our reaction to how we are feeling about ourselves? Our reaction on a good day may be to laugh and maybe take a nap. Our reaction on a not so good day is no laughing matter. The cumulative effect on our self-esteem is devastating.

Unravelling the tangled mess of wires in my thinking meant studying the difference between those who ride the self-defeat train and those who did not let circumstances derail them. What I saw was astoundingly simple. Those who were the most confident in themselves did not allow much rattle them.

Great. Confidence is the answer. But how do I do that? Becoming confident is a process that starts with the refusal to believe the garbage we tell ourselves daily. It means choosing faith and acceptance of yourself just as you are over the fear of what others may think about you.

It means embracing every part of you and seeing beauty in all your humanity, warts and all. It means saying nice things to yourself when no one is listening. It means looking beyond the reflection in the mirror and ending the crippling "if I had only done this, or should not have done that, things would be different" internal dialogue. Confidence is the reward when we call bullshit on that inner voice and see it for what it is: a big fat liar.

That critical voice lies in wait for those who are in pain, heartbroken, or experiencing chaos and often takes root at a young age. These rumblings of self-doubt or insecurity give birth to the voice that tells us we are not smart enough, thin enough, pretty enough, or perfect enough to be able to claim our place in the world. Our units of measurement become incorrect assessments of what is "good" and "bad" and clouds our view of ourselves and the world.

In my work as a wellness coach, one of my biggest pet peeves was clients referencing whether they had been "good" or "bad" with their food choices. How we label ourselves and our behavior creates a mindset of failure right out of the gate. Choices are neutral. What we eat is how we fuel our body. While some choices are better than others, none determine our worth. Shifting the mindset about our choices helps circumvent the baggage we associate with good or bad. "I was bad this weekend and ate fried chicken" colors the perception of self. "I ate junk this weekend" is a more accurate statement of fact which is free from self-judgement and negative thinking.

If we are not vigilant about keeping this kind of sabotage at bay, it will block us from receiving the good things we all deserve. The critical voice serves no purpose other than allowing negativity the power to continue calling the shots and wearing us out. The origins of that voice are of little consequence in changing how we see ourselves. We can be our own worst critics at times, but this is not okay.

Believing in our perceived shortcomings and allowing them to shape our self-image and determine our behavior is unacceptable. Working on becoming our own biggest fan takes much less energy than it does to criticize and beat ourselves up. Trust me. Let go of the belief that what we do determines who we are. These are two very separate things. Who we are, at times, does influence the things we do. However, our value and worth are not predicated on what we do. Value and worth are inherent in our being and are independent of anything we do.

REPUTATION

When my oldest son graduated from high school, a school board member spoke at commencement. Mixed with the usual dream big and work hard messages was wisdom about the importance of students protecting their reputations as they ventured into the world. This sentiment was met with spontaneous applause from many in attendance. Yes, all the old folks, me included, understood this priceless advice for the graduating class of 2016.

He spoke about respecting themselves and being mindful of how they moved through the world. Their actions mattered. How they conducted themselves mattered. He encouraged them to be thoughtful about everything they did and said. The world keeps track of how people behave.

Hang on while I climb off my dinosaur and put down my brontosaurus burger. Back in the day, we would rather die than leave any possible evidence of wrongdoing. The unspoken rule of surviving childhood, and our questionable decision-making skills, was to avoid leaving tangible proof at all costs.

No photos, video, or even written words were allowed. We would rather eat paper and ink than get caught in possession of an incriminating note. Video cameras were the size of microwaves and completely outside of our access. Polaroid cameras were the enemy.

We survived because of the unspoken honor code and understood when one was snagged, we all suffered dings to our backsides and reputations. We had a firm grasp on the importance of staying off the hoodlum list in our neighborhood.

Getting removed from that list was nearly impossible unless you moved away and started over somewhere else. The awareness of how we would be seen by adults or those outside of our inner circle was a definite concern.

There are countless avenues for sharing today. Thanks to social media and technology, endless opportunities for sharing and documenting our lives exist. While not a bad thing in and of itself, there can be consequences when we impulsively react to situations, share too much personal information, or document behavior that may bite us in the ass or damage our reputation.

I am right there with those who may be wondering where I get the nerve to talk about oversharing after writing a memoir about coming out later in life. I get it. Any who have read *Switching Teams* will notice there is plenty I did not say. Some have expressed disappointment about not finding enough drama within the pages. Side note to self: You can't please everyone.

Naturally, I was concerned about how I would be perceived, judged, and evaluated. I was mindful of the beliefs or opinions that would result from my words being published, which is the definition of reputation by the way. Private moments, details, and memories were intentionally omitted from the final draft not out of fear, but out of necessity. Sure, it may have provided a more sordid tale or more interesting reading, but it did not add to the message.

Like it or not, our reputation is how the world views us. It is a measure of our character and our emotions can become stirred up when we realize people are picking up exactly what we are putting out. Ouch. Behaving in ways that contradict who we are projects an inaccurate picture to those around us and can result in pain, sadness, or feeling disconnected from the world.

Paying appropriate attention to how our behavior may be perceived is a check and balance for authenticity but is not the same as conforming to how others think we should be in order to be accepted by them.

Authenticity is being comfortable with every part of who we are. A good reputation can cover over a multitude of sins, mitigate mistakes, and show our ability to recover from lapses in judgment.

Moving Through

If we look at a reputation as something we are responsible for creating and maintaining internally, what others see will match our true selves.

Presenting the most genuine version of ourselves may be scary at times, but it is a practice that will never fail us, or those around us. This is what I heard while sitting in the graduation ceremony. Translation: Love yourself and good things follow.

Making certain we are sharing our most authentic selves with the world requires us to edit at times. If character is a crayon, reputation is the coloring book. I encourage you to take a moment and scan the completed coloring book pages pinned to your walls. Who do you see? Is love present? Love breeds good decisions and confidence, which in turn creates fertile reputation grounds.

Be gentle but honest in your assessment of areas which may need improvement and celebrate the hell out of the areas where you are kicking ass. As I climb back on my dinosaur, I remind you to breathe and trust that at this moment you are exactly where you are supposed to be.

Milling about acting like we are less than another is robbing us of our amazing potential. Sharing our varied gifts, talents, and abilities makes our world interesting and give us opportunities to relate to one another with hope and understanding.

GET YOUR MIND RIGHT

While I have never been a die-hard movie aficionado, I do have a list of favorites. Included in my top ten are Mars Attacks, Little Miss

Love Yourself

Sunshine, Beetlejuice, Dead Calm, and Silence of the Lambs. I appreciate twisted plot lines, ridiculous humor, and movies that most serious movie critics would throw up in their mouths over.

While my taste in movies may be suspect to some, I do appreciate many mainstream classics and enjoy movie quotes. Two of my favorites are from the 1967 Paul Newman movie Cool Hand Luke. *"You run one time, you got yourself a set of chain. You run twice you got yourself two sets. You ain't gonna need no third set, 'cause you gonna get your mind right."* What does this mean? This simple exchange is a reminder of how thinking affects our actions. Specifically, negative thinking creates negative reactions.

Getting our minds right is a process that begins with examining how we view the world, others, and most importantly, ourselves. I suspect each of us experiences moments of getting our mind right multiple times throughout the day. We may not even realize it is happening. Think about the last time you felt like things were going off the rails. Was it something someone else did to you? What did you do to right the ship? How quickly were you able to recover?

We may naturally conclude the issue is with someone else and fail to look beneath the surface of our reaction. I learned long ago that I have very little control over what others do or say. I also learned my reactions are closely tied to how I am feeling about myself on any given day. We get caught up in the drama or emotion of the reaction and make it about the other person. On the surface it seems that our problems lie squarely in the laps of others.

If they would just stop it, we would be fine. It is easy to point the finger at someone else when conflict happens. We all do it. I need not look further than this election cycle for examples. It is often a knee jerk reaction and our first line of defense when we feel like we are being attacked. Let's be honest, sometimes people are just assholes. The other, less popular side of the coin relates to the flawed view of self that many struggle with. Put simply, our internal dialogue impacts how we react to the world around us.

Low self-esteem and negative self-talk are quiet little monsters, which, left unchecked, can creep in and destroy all that could be good in our lives. How many of us stop and think about why whatever they have said or done is affecting us so negatively? This is a tough topic for me to tackle. This hit close to home on many levels. Low self-esteem is an often-understated problem and the effects can be devastating on a variety of fronts.

There are many causes of low self-esteem. Recognizing the root cause is an important step in overcoming the challenges but is not a cure all. I spent many years feeling inadequate, unworthy, and just plain shitty. When I got to the root of this thinking, I was relieved, however nothing changed. Knowing why did not change anything, it just made me angry. Those pesky questions again. I realized, after many tantrums, the only way out of the cycle of negative self-talk was to reprogram my inner dialogue.

For years, my internal state constantly seeped out externally. Garbage inside, garbage out. I took everything personally, not because it was true or real, but because my negative script colored every page of my adult coloring book. Self-acceptance began when it struck me that I would never talk to anyone as harshly as I talked to myself. This was my turning point. My filter needed to be changed. My priority was to view myself the way my family and friends did and to begin to put my faith in what they said instead of what I told myself. I reprogrammed my default button and my life took off in ways that I never imagined possible.

Many years ago, my aunt sent an article about that little voice in our heads that tells us we are flawed, that our failings can never be forgiven, and that we are not worthy of good things. The author named her little voice Stan. Her way of dealing with that little nagging voice was to say, "Shut Up Stan."

We all have moments of low self-esteem. How we react and choose to move through them are critical to keeping a healthy and positive mind. Shut up Stan. One moment, if not addressed and reframed with the truth of who we are, can turn into a downward spiral. We use the opinions of others to build a case against ourselves which feeds the monster. Shut Up Stan.

When our minds are right, the opinions of others do not matter, and things are more apt to roll off our backs. Athletes are notorious for struggling with negative self-talk, which is why many professional athletes engage the services of sports psychologists to help them keep their minds right. Their goal is to remain in a positive head space so they can perform and be their very best. Isn't this the goal for each of us?

One formula does not exist to squash negative self-talk or overcome low self-esteem. No magic pill can be prescribed to remedy the problem. Paying attention to how we speak to ourselves helps highlight the damage negative self-talk has on relationships, success, and overall happiness.

Do not be afraid to ask for help or support in any avenue that you feel drawn to personally. Sometimes we need others to remind us of our true selves and to help break through the razor wire fence. When you see someone struggling, be kind. Remind them of the truth of who they are, despite what they may be thinking. This is one instance when interrupting the electrical circuit turns on the light. As you move through and address whatever struggle you may be having, trust the process and resist fighting the growing pains. You are worth it.

Admittedly, I spent many years under a blanket of anger. It was not until I married and began my family that I realized this state of mind was destructive. My anger and resentment served no other purpose than to perpetuate the negative internal dialogue playing in my brain. It told me loudly that I did not matter, that I was not important, and that I was not good enough. It screamed at me whenever I got close to accomplishing something amazing.

It whispered reminders in my quiet moments that, no matter what, I could never be ok or do anything important or meaningful. There were many demons to contend with. How I saw myself was very unhealthy. Thanks therapy.

I was frustrated. It seemed like it was taking forever for me to feel like I was fixed. I was encouraged to journal, which produced some amazing rants and raves, but never got the root out of the ground.

Al Anon helped, but more would rise to the surface as I continued the process of finding the source of discontent with myself. Venting helped but felt unproductive. I still felt like a curly haired nothing wearing sneakers.

One day, I unleashed my anger into the universe via a piece of paper and a pen in a frantic attempt to be rid of this smoldering angst. The result was my most pitiful journal entry of all time. Writing heals. This was the beginning of the end of my own self destruction and loathing. I could see colors other than red and understood living under a cloud of the past was no way to live. Getting to that angry place and allowing myself to feel it without interference from my own self-protective walls was a huge step and the beginning of me handling my shit. Being "fixed" was my goal and it seemed unattainable.

Black and white thinking sabotaged my journey. Things were either broken or fixed. There were no gray areas. The realization that "fixing" yourself is not like repairing a flat tire was a light bulb moment. The bottom line was I saw myself as flawed. Why it was flawed mattered but changing the thinking which got me there was more important. This shift in thinking happened slowly and quietly. There was no fanfare. I was just ready to let go of the horrific self-image I had created and wanted nothing more than to rebuild the self-esteem that I had not allowed myself to accept.

I was elated when I was finally able to reject this thinking. It was stifling and painful. It made life seem too dark most of the time. One evening, not long after confessing my feelings to Yvette, I recognized that thinking this way was ridiculous and a waste of time. Every day since has been different. The secret was simple. I decided to get out of my own way and truly begin to look at myself and stop blaming life for my issues. By no means did this fix me. Sifting through the lingering stinking thinking and remembering to get out of your own way is hard when life seems unfair or the "you don't matter" buttons are pushed.

The conversation in my head is something I closely monitor. Remembering I am ok exactly how I am in any given moment or in any circumstance does the trick. I challenge you to take a moment and imagine how it would feel if, for one day, you sent the critic packing. Just one day. Baby steps. This may be as simple as forgiving yourself for whatever keeps the itty-bitty shitty committee in session. It is as simple as letting go of the ridiculous notion of perfection and embracing ourselves exactly as we are. It means remembering the important things and becoming as gentle with ourselves as we are with others. Ouch. I said it.

With time, practice, and a little help from our friends, that voice will be quieted and what will remain is peace. What have you done for yourself today? If nothing, I suggest taking a minute to remember how amazing you are. If you are having one of those days, call a friend and they will help you out. Defer to their judgment for the day and give yourself a break.

Loving yourself is a decision to embrace the total package. The first step is different for everyone but starts with adopting a kinder and gentler way of thinking about ourselves. It begins with rejecting harsh thoughts and replacing them with loving ones. It may even mean faking it until you make it.

Love Yourself

As you maneuver through your own winding road, do not be afraid to feel the hard things and admit when you are struggling. Bad days happen. Mistakes happen. Life happens. Love yourself anyway. Resist the temptation to retreat and shrink down when choosing yourself and joy is not met with applause from everyone else. Be proud of who you are and loving yourself will become second nature. You will wonder how it was possible for you to feel anything other than love for yourself all this time.

Remember that love, for yourself or another person, is the most important variable in the equation of peace. Embracing the truth about the great things we bring to the world opens the door to finding purpose and living a life with meaning and joy.

20 - FINDING PURPOSE

Shifting our thinking away from others and toward loving ourselves fiercely is the precursor to figuring out our purpose. How many can say they know what their purpose is? For some it is an abstract concept. Stop for a minute and ponder the possibility of purpose being a dynamic concept. Every moment brings new opportunities for creating purpose. Purpose is not static. Purpose changes as the life cycle progresses. A child's purpose is to be a child. To learn, grow, and evolve into an eventual adult.

In the adult world, purpose can be as simple as being a kind human. Finding our purpose is a lesson in flexibility as things change. Purpose is a multifaceted entity. It is part of what allows us to contribute our unique mark to the world. As life unfolds, purpose can shift. How we go about the business of defining our purpose is up to each individual. There are no rules but when purpose is lacking, problems arise.

In a relationship, purpose is often confused with expectation and obligation. Add this to the list of roadblocks. The roles individuals

Finding Purpose

play in their lives can easily be confused with deep purpose. Parsing through the roadblocks to our own authenticity helps bring our purpose in to view. Purpose is uniquely personal and cannot be decided by anyone other than ourselves.

As we age, finding purpose becomes an important part of creating a meaningful and fulfilling life. Changes are the bosom buddies of purpose. Although uncomfortable, change can be a powerful tool for discovering purpose in life. When I began writing this book, my purpose was to go deeper in the pool of authenticity. The purpose of challenging myself and committing to sharing even more of myself was to help others understand and embrace their authentic selves.

Coming out later in life was a change which sparked the desire to help others who were feeling alone in their journey. Becoming a widow at the age of 47 was not something I planned for. What was the purpose in that? Purpose can shift as we respond to the events of life.

How interesting would be to go back in time and interview our five-year-old selves? I would ask what she wanted to be when she grew up. I would also ask about her hopes for the future. I would also ask her what she thought her purpose was.

Even though I was there, it was a long time ago. As a child, purpose was not on my radar unless you count figuring out how to convince my parents to let me eat ice cream for dinner. I do remember having goals. My goal was to be Quincy MD, a pilot, an astronaut, or a baseball player. Future hopes included not having a bedtime and eating ice cream whenever I wanted. That is how five-year old's roll right?

Fortunately, old report cards, yearbooks, and greeting cards gave me a glimpse of how my teachers, coaches, and peers viewed me. By understanding who we are and dealing with our baggage in healthy ways, we clear the path of obstacles and purpose emerges.

Becoming who I am today was a product of the experiences, opportunities, obstacles, and challenges in my life. The intersection of these elements created and formed how I think, feel, and behave. My purpose shifted as the years progressed and became simplified. Helping others while loving myself fiercely throughout my journey is a broad purpose. Knowing who I am and sharing my story is one way I fulfill my purpose. Keeping fear at bay and being authentic helps keep me honest. Being amenable to change and learning to adapt to the unexpected turns life brings is helpful as well.

Before Yvette died, we created a group on Facebook called Married Lesbian Life. Up until then, our search for a non-hook up, authentic, and encouraging place where we could connect with other married lesbian couples was unsuccessful. Building a community of lesbian married folks was the answer.

Marriage, gay or straight, is a journey with many highs and lows. The purpose was to create a safe space where other lesbian couples were free to celebrate their marriages and spouses, offer support, and feel a sense of belonging. Easy example, right?

Looking for a deeper purpose in the story takes us back to coming out. Our lesbian life timeline is shorter than most. We came out later

Finding Purpose

in life and were both previously married to men. *Switching Teams* included an entire chapter about labels, stereotypes, and a discussion regarding the struggle to be accepted as "real" lesbians given our historically hetero past.

As such, copious amounts of time and energy have been spent, publicly and privately, fielding inquiries about why it took so long to figure out we were gay or, better yet, how someone could be completely unaware of such a huge part of themselves.

For a long time, my purpose became finding the words to explain this. I became an expert in evading giving an answer to this question. Not because I am uncomfortable talking about my life, but because I had yet to construct an adequate response that erased the confused look from whomever asked. My Dawn and I have discussed this at length. I had no clue, while she had some idea that she was a lesbian when she married him.

When pressed, I chose to respond with humor. I also capitalized on the opportunity for a teaching moment to reinforce the lesson of remaining in the present moment or the idea that knowing why was not as important as moving forward. There was truth to that, but the high-level psychobabble approach was nothing more than a slick way to avoid looking unprepared or uninformed.

Crafting a coherent explanation for how my lesbian realization escaped me for forty years was high on my list of things to do for the past eight years. Despite spending countless hours of self-interrogation, brow beating, and wading through every moment of my life up until I came out, a satisfactory reason had yet to surface.

Moving Through

A friendly inquiry from a fellow member of the Married Lesbian Life group challenged me to finally figure out how to explain the lack of awareness. Wrestling with what has become life's most nagging dilemma is not a one sentence answer. The answer is simple, yet oh so complicated. First things first.

Looking for an answer means you must decide whether it is important enough to spend time and energy milling through missed signs, wading through your past, and digging emotional ditches with only a spoon. You also must be willing to accept the possibility that some may never understand.

In a perfect world, everyone would know everything about themselves from the moment they were born. We could all skip through life holding hands and making a joyful noise throughout all creation. Barf. Back to reality.

Knowing our authentic selves is not a straight-line process and is influenced by events, people, places, and our experiences. Each of these interactions deposits layers on our lives. The residue can be thick or thin, transparent or opaque, quiet or loud.

Every layer colors our thoughts, emotions, physical being, or sense of who we are and how we do things. Think wallpaper. My internal décor was wallpapered to the hilt. The rainbow paper was hidden beneath decades of poor decorating choices.

Dealing with anxiety, fear, low self-esteem, anger, and feeling like something was wrong with me kept me busy. Figuring out my true sexual orientation was never even on the radar.

Finding Purpose

Getting down to the studs took some time to accomplish. In my case, I did not realize my truth earlier because my attention was focused only on the visible layer and not what was underneath.

As a child, I was sheltered and the most pressing concerns in my life were likely about how to create the perfect pocket in my baseball glove or which pair of sneakers to wear. Homosexuality was not a frequently discussed issue in my extremely Catholic neighborhood or home.

I was a tomboy who had boyfriends and never questioned my sexuality. I was always more comfortable being one of the guys because I felt like I did not fit in or have anything in common with other girls.

Despite having deeply emotional relationships with a few women in college, I was never physically attracted to any of them. Being gay is all about who you have sex with, right? An opportunity to "explore" would not have helped because I was not questioning my sexuality. Everything else about me, yes, but sexual orientation, no.

Until 2006, I had never been asked outright if I was gay or straight. Not once. Ever. At the time, I was married with three children under the age of ten and was beginning to take serious steps to toward dissecting the accumulated baggage and layers in my life. My reaction to the question raised some alarms.

Meeting my first wife was a powerful moment and helped me find my truth. Timing is everything. As my mindset and sense of self shifted in a healthy way, the core of my unrest surfaced, and I began to connect the dots and entertain the idea I was gay.

The short answer to the original question is this. Knowing and embracing our authentic selves and finding purpose is a lifelong activity. Our journey toward discovering important things about who we are happens when we are ready to hear the message. Enlightenment happens when it is supposed to happen. Purpose follows.

Admittedly, I wasted time wishing I would have known when I was younger, and I too share in the disbelief many expressed to me. Seriously. I get it. Sure, looking back, there were signs. There always are. Hello regret.

However, the choice to resist dwelling on the "what if" and "how could I not have" is my path forward. Honestly, if given the choice to go back and redo things I would decline the offer. Changing the past would alter the now. My purpose has become authentic living. Today I am grateful for hindsight which I now view as a validation for my truth instead of a condemnation for what I did not know then. The delay in my self-actualization was a prime example of when mindfulness is not a priority.

21 - MINDFULNESS

What is mindfulness? It is the quality or state of being mindful, which is not the most helpful explanation. A more descriptive definition is the practice of maintaining a nonjudgmental state of heightened or complete awareness of one's thoughts, emotions, or experiences on a moment-to-moment basis.

Now we are getting somewhere. Whether at work or play, mindfulness can be challenging if you regularly seek out constant activity and stimulation. Having a full mind and being mindful are not the same thing. It is difficult to believe mindfulness will work when feelings of anger, sadness, or fear are bubbling inside.

Remaining present means paying attention to not only the tasks which need to be completed but also how we are feeling, thinking, and behaving in the moment. Finding the sources of negative self-talk and patterns of old behavior which are rooted in the past are also included. Learning to slow down and be present is a skill requiring both practice and patience.

Moving Through

Many steps and changes may be necessary before true mindfulness is possible. Circumstances or situations which create a full mind are around every corner. We have been conditioned to believe idle minds belong in the same category of hell as idle hands. Thoughtful, slow, and deliberate living can be viewed by some as a weakness or a flaw. Who has time to be mindful?

Today, people must be constantly thinking, creating, or performing in order to be successful or productive. Busy is the new black. Being bored can feel unsettling for many who have become reliant upon technology to constantly occupy the mind. Busyness is also a great way to avoid dealing with issues which prevent us from living a peace filled life.

One night my family was discussing the merits of meditation and mindfulness. Explaining how mindfulness works was a challenge. The consensus was that mindfulness does not work. Mindfulness is more than emptying the brain of any thoughts. The brain is always working. Clearing the mind of everything is an impossibility. Mindfulness is the act of keeping your mind on the present moment and focusing on one activity. It is also allowing intrusive thoughts to happen but letting them pass through without further analysis.

Downtime happens only when sleep comes. Well, not really. It has been shown that sleep and health are affected when the brain does not have an opportunity to wind down before going to bed. On or off is not how we were meant to exist.

One day, I took a tumble down my stairs. Only a few bruises to show for it, the biggest one to my ego. For an unfortunate moment, my mind wandered at the top of the staircase. My socked feet hit the stair wrong and I ended up flat on my ass. You're welcome for that visual. After the shock wore off, I was angry for being such an idiot and for not being mindful of what I was doing in that moment.

Is this an extreme example? Maybe. Does it illustrate the importance of balance? Absolutely. Both literally and figuratively. Enter Balance. A lack of mindfulness upsets equilibrium and creates obstacles on our staircases. Chaos is an indicator that balance is faltering. Work. Home. Family. Obligations.

LEARNING TO BE MINDFUL.

Busy minds are productive but also create chaos, exhaustion, and conflict at home, work, or play. Practicing mindfulness helps create a more positive and peaceful energy for us individually and in our home. Meditation is one way to learn mindfulness, however it can be as simple as noticing rising anxiety and stopping to pay attention the feeling. It passes when you acknowledge it. Worry is the enemy of mindfulness.

Mindfulness is not problem solving, overthinking, or looking for answers. It is feeling while being in the moment. Failing to deal with lingering emotions or feelings has a cumulative effect on the internal noise level within.

Mindfulness helps to lower the volume and heal. Try breathing, exercise, or just sitting in the quiet. Find what works for you and go with that. There are no wrong answers when it comes to minding your thoughts. Freeing up this valuable space within is the key to peace. Some practice yoga or use exercise to practice being mindful. Others climb mountains or sit in dark rooms.

Be patient with yourself in the beginning. Commit to doing one thing every day which helps focus on the present moment. Be intentional about the things you give attention to. Awareness is the first step toward reducing stress and improving your mental health and well-being.

The key to mindfulness begins with balance. Finding the balance between work and rest is a common theme for many people. Our vehicles are either speeding down the highway or tucked away under a cover in the garage. Spending time considering ways to better operate within the space and scope of moderation builds mindfulness. Planning for moderation is easy but adopting the practice of it is another story. Achieving balance is the ultimate prize.

First things first. What does it mean to be "in balance?" It depends on who you ask and what you are referring to. My favorite definition is a condition in which different elements are equal or in the correct proportions. Now we are getting somewhere.

Being able to walk down the street without falling over is one example. If balance is off, we might fall over. Thinking about the word in this light gives a visual representation of what happens inside of us when the elements in our lives are not equal or in correct proportion.

Balance is a multidimensional concept. The summer after Yvette was diagnosed with cancer, we decided to take some time off to regroup and relax. The goal was to renew our minds, bodies, and spirits and to perfect the art of balance. The universe met our determination with plenty of opportunities to practice. Thanks universe.

Our first attempt was an abject failure. Just a friendly tip. If you are trying to reset the balance meter, scheduling doctor appointments is not recommended. In a three-day period, two cancer scares began which amped up the chaos. Note to self: survival mode is an extreme.

We did not abort the mission, but this added additional challenges to our search for balance. The only thing that grounded us was our conscious decision to focus of gratitude. Nonetheless, we persisted. It was not pretty or graceful. During this experiment we learned a few things. Balance is not a static process. It is a dynamic one. Announcing intentions to the universe is the easy part. Achieving balance is an active process which requires more thought and effort than birthing a child.

MIND, BODY, SPIRIT CONNECTION

The most valuable lesson I learned as a personal trainer was the relationship between balancing the mind, body, and spirit.

Our bodies are in a constant quest for homeostasis, which is the fancy word for balance. When one element is off, the body searches for ways to correct it. The process of maintaining homeostasis can cause damage and create issues with other systems. Hello high blood pressure, weight gain, and metabolic changes.

These changes alter how the body works and subsequently how we feel, think, or behave. Sound familiar? Working at the expense of family or unplugging and hiding from reality have the same effect and outcome. All or nothing without any room for the middle ground is a red flag.

There is a time and place for all things. Spend some quiet time considering where balance improvements can be made in your life. If you are feeling tired, depressed, or anxious, chances are some areas might need adjustments.

SELF CARE

When anxiety and fear surface, it indicates something within us is being stirred. Learning to adjust how we react to fear is a lifelong lesson and at the root of balance. It is easy to find peace when nothing is blowing up and all seems right in the world. These are the moments when gratitude reigns. Resist the urge to be suspicious or to wait for the shoe to drop. Taking time to step back, pause, and plug in to our emotions and mental state is the key to practicing self-care. Self-care is often confused with selfishness. Self-care aids our growth and creates positive energy in our lives.

Saying no is a highly underutilized method of self-care. Overextending ourselves creates tension and shifts our focus away from maintaining balance. It is acceptable to say no and to choose yourself over others without explanation. Those who are healthy will appreciate the no. Those who argue or demand an explanation have not gotten there yet.

Self-care is anything which recharges our batteries when life becomes overwhelming. Choosing self-care is an important piece of the wellness puzzle. Whether the focus is on the mind, body or spirit is of no consequence. There is no virtue in sacrificing self for the sake of promoting peace for another. Anything which works against our own wellness guarantees misery. Life is short and living in misery is a consummate waste of precious time. Begin with mindfulness and remember overhauling everything is not the first step in the process. Set some goals and hash out a plan which will bring balance to the areas of your life that are the most out of whack. Recognizing the importance of slowing down and reducing chaos is step one.

GRATITUDE

Once mindfulness and balance have been activated, the next step is looking for opportunities to practice gratitude. Start with the obvious. If you are stuck, look around your home at the people and things that mean the most to you. Turn on the television. There are plenty of reminders of things to be grateful for there. Be grateful for the moments when you learn something new or witness an act of random kindness from a stranger.

Mastering balance can be exhausting in the beginning. Mindfulness is the caffeine boost for balance. Gratitude is the whipped cream on the balance latte. Without either we lean and lose our footing.

Once mindfulness begins to grow, maintaining balance becomes less taxing on our systems. Thinking about what you are doing, how you are feeling, or how you are behaving is part one. Enter gratitude. What does the act of being grateful have to do with learning to keep balance? Everything. Gratitude neutralizes chaos from the inside out.

It is nearly impossible to be grateful and consumed by chaos simultaneously. Gratitude helps balance the scales and focuses our minds on the important things in life. It taps the brakes on speeding thoughts and actions. It also jumpstarts dead batteries in broken down vehicles.

Thankfulness does not always get enough credit for its power to restore balance in our lives. Being mindful of the little things helps the big things seem less overwhelming. As you practice these steps, peace will begin to replace the chaos and the seesaw will begin to right itself. Taking a break does not mean we are unproductive and working constantly is no guarantee of success. Also, taking time is not an invitation for bad things to happen. Shocking. Balance. The lessons are everywhere.

There is a time and place for everything. Continue to be gentle with yourself as you work toward balancing the areas of your life which need attention. Start with a list if you are overwhelmed with where to begin. When you fall, brush yourself off, get back up and keep going forward. Take heart and be grateful that the bruises are temporary.

22 - PENNIES FROM HEAVEN

Before my wife died, she thought the spirit world was "a bunch of shit." I did not share her opinion. Despite her lack of confidence in the spirit world, she was a fan of television shows about hauntings, ghosts, and communicating with deceased loved ones. Jokingly, I would instruct any spirits around us to mess with her. I was a believer and she needed convincing. We promised if something ever happened to one of us, the other would seek out a medium to try to connect to the beyond. We even had a code word to use to make sure it was legit.

Soon after she passed, I began my search for a medium to settle the dispute over who was right. She liked to be right, and usually was. The belief that loved ones merely transition to another plane when they die is not shared by everyone. My own opinion centered on the idea that there were elements of the universe which human beings were unable to comprehend. Remaining open to the existence of the spirit world was never a stretch for me.

Moving Through

If you are in the "bunch of shit" camp, this is for you.

My first attempt to connect was at the end of February during a group reading with a medium. Colby Rebel is a nationally recognized medium and she made an appearance at The Venue in Orlando. I went in with an open mind and had no expectations about what, if anything, I would walk away with. My hope was to find out if she was at peace and okay.

Colby performed 8 or 9 readings during the hour and a half group reading session that night. I figured if there were ever a place for her to come through, this would be it. I asked my friend Helen to go with me for moral support. Whether or not she came through, it was nice to be out of the house and spending time with a dear friend. We settled in and the group readings began.

The fourth reading of the night began with a mention of a sister figure or best friend stepping forward. I thought nothing of it. Then she began to mention things that got my attention. Cancer. Fund raiser. Stubborn. Fighter. Dancing. Promises. The lady in front of me thought it was a friend of hers and claimed it. As the medium kept sharing, she stopped talking to the lady and pointed in my direction and asked if any of this made sense to me. I was floored. My friend realized it was her well before it registered for me. I raised my hand, took the mic, and said I understood.

I spoke few words other than to validate what she was saying. At one point the medium just stopped and said "okay, okay, okay" while pacing. My wife was a persistent woman and was in overdrive. I had to laugh. She described her as compassionate, kind, loving, and someone who was always there for people. Nailed it.

She described our relationship as inseparable and close. I told her she was my wife. Remember how adamant she was about me keeping my promises to her? The medium mentioned it four times. Message received. Through her I was able to connect and get the message thanking me for never leaving her side and for always being there for her.

As the medium was wrapping up, she mentioned a signature or handwriting and asked if that made sense to me. I confirmed the tattoo of her handwriting on my arm. I was wearing a long sleeve shirt and got it a month after she passed. It was the words "Moving Though..." which I copied from her list of possible titles for her show.

Mediums tend to pace and gesture while someone is coming through. At the end of the reading, she walked to the end of the stage and stood still. The words "I love you" came out of her mouth. I got goose bumps.

When she finished, I texted the keywords to my phone to remember what just happened. I stared at the floor for a moment and then looked at my friend. On the table was a penny. Neither of us placed it there. Our phones were the only items on the table that night. Without question. The penny was not there. Then it was. No explanation.

It was an amazing night. Whether or not you believe in the spirit world, there is no disputing our loved ones are with us. On the way home, I opened a Spotify playlist and hit shuffle. The first seven songs that played all meant something to us. I turned off the music because it was too much. Persistent wife strikes again. I laughed and said out loud "Okay, I got it. I can only handle so much Yvette."

In the days after her death, I began finding pennies in strange places. I mentioned it to my hair stylist, and she was shocked to learn I had never heard of the "pennies from heaven" phenomenon. Every penny found was heads up. I was intrigued. There is no scientific explanation for how a penny can materialize and appear out of the blue. In the spirit world, pennies, or sometimes dimes, are a sign someone is trying to communicate with you. Finding them outside of the ordinary places one would expect to find a penny gets our attention.

Mission accomplished. Opening the refrigerator and seeing one on the bottom shelf got my attention. Glancing at an empty dining room table one moment and finding two pennies at the places where we used to sit had my attention. The shower shelf, dashboard of my car, and in the bathtub of the guest bath all were noticed. Explaining the penny scourge to my youngest was met with a "why doesn't she leave hundreds?" Comedy heals.

The most memorable penny story happened when we decided to sell her car. My son was not old enough to drive and our driveway space was limited. We posted it for sale and the phone rang an hour later. It was an uncle inquiring about the car. He shared that his nephew lost his father to cancer when he was twelve. This even got Dawn's attention. She also lost a parent at the age of twelve. What would Yvette do? I agreed to sell it for less than it was listed to work

Pennies from Heaven

within their budget. When they arrived for the test drive, the car was completely cleared out. The young man took it for a spin and returned without incident. He exited the car and I waited for him to get the cash out of his car.

Feeling nostalgic, I took one last look inside and saw a penny on the center console. My heart skipped. I tried to get Dawn's attention to confirm what I was seeing. The way I tried to casually ask her to come look at something alarmed the young couple. They were afraid something was wrong with the car. No. Everything was right. Message received.

A month later, I attended a private reading with medium in Orlando. My meeting with Heidi Jaffe was scheduled a few weeks after she died. My decision to keep the appointment, despite hearing her come through at the group reading, was wise. The private reading brought more than I ever expected in the way of healing and messages from beyond. She began with an explanation of how spirit spoke to her. Then took a deep breath and began counting. One. Two. Three. Four. Five. Six. Seven. Seven?

Seven of my deceased family stepped forward. Three from the maternal side on her right, three from the paternal side on her left, and one very loud spirit who was next to me on the couch. She began with the maternal side. My great grandmother, who suffered from Alzheimer's disease, my grandmother, and grandfather. She identified them by first name. Mary, Eleanor, and John. Their message was about forgiveness and healing. On the paternal side, my stepmom, who died from cancer a day before Yvette had her double mastectomy, came through. My dad's brother and his wife who both passed from cancer also came through. Again, she identified their initials.

Then she got around to the "insistent" female energy next to me. I knew it was Yvette. She was eerily specific about every detail. The message was much more personal than the group reading. I was thanked for staying by her side and for taking care of her. She described her eyes and her shock about how quickly everything unraveled. Cancer. Sepsis. All spot on.

The medium told me Yvette communicates with pennies and music. Bingo. Pennies? I almost fell off the couch. Heidi also said "Some who passed on will send people to those left behind. She is saying she could have been mean and sent someone exactly like her, but instead she sent you someone who was a little less chaotic. Does this make sense?"

"Yes."

The exact wording was important here. This validated my suspicion she may have had something to do with the unexpected new person appearing in my life. Message received.

My third experience was another group reading with Colby Rebel a year after the second reading with Heidi. The Venue was again the location. I took Dawn with me this time. Date night for the bereft. The attendance was larger than the first group reading so I my expectations were low about hearing from Yvette again. Truthfully, I hoped Dawn's father would come through. He was a veteran and police officer who was killed in a car accident during a police chase when she was twelve.

Pennies from Heaven

Sure as shit, the fourth reading began with the mention of a "strong sister energy" coming forward. I knew it was her. The wording was exactly how she described her the last time. I knew. Unbeknownst to me, a woman she worked with was recording the reading from the front row. First up was the mention of two rings. The recording is something I listened to many times.

> "Do two rings make sense? Or double rings?"
>
> "Yes."

Before we left the house, I pulled out two rings Yvette had given me. I asked Dawn which one went better with my outfit. What followed was a humorous exchange. By this time the microphone was in my hands.

She continued and then paused saying:

> "Oh. No. I can't just say that. I will say it exactly as I heard it so you will have to forgive me."

I said, "Go ahead, just say it."

Laughter.

> "Would you understand her thinking she is smarter than you?"
>
> "Yes"
>
> "Ok. And that when she was right about an argument you never heard the end of it."
>
> "Yes."
>
> "She just loved to rub that in."
>
> "Yes."
>
> "She is also giving me something about her feet, I don't know if it is her feet or your feet. Do one of you have big ole feet?"
>
> "Yes. That would be me."

Laughter.

"And you would make her rub those feet or something like that? Is that right?"

"Yes."

"She wasn't a fond person of feet, but she rubbed them because she loves you. She also understands, she makes me feel like she is ill before she passes or a sense of cancer. Is that correct?"

"Yep."

"Also, it is so weird because did it go down her back? Or something? She makes me feel like it went all the way down my spine. She makes me feel like her body was not functioning. I think her speech got slurred. Or something with her mouth as well. Her mouth was lopsided toward the end. Do you understand what I am referring to?"

"Yeah."

"Okay. I think that there's dribble coming out and she wants to thank you for cleaning up the dribble. I just don't think you left her side and just feel like you were constantly there, and she needed strong medical care. Again, I think she is slipping into a coma. And I am not sure so you can correct me if I am wrong but I feel like you are kind of almost shouting or in a panic to tell them to "Give her more medicine give her more medicine!" but you did not realize she could hear you. She wants you to know she could hear you. And she is like "well you don't even know what she was saying about the medicine but there were a few choice words coming out of her mind as to give me that medicine as well. And so, I feel like she keeps saying thank you thank you thank you. You kissed, it's weird, normally I see a kiss on the cheek, this one is weird, but I see a kiss on the eyelids or right up here. She knows you did that. So, at that point she is letting you know that was her goodbye. Either she had just passed she is showing me from above you. She is letting me know to thank you for it. I don't think you like all her family people and she wants to thank you for being patient with them and for connecting with them and talking with them. She just lets me know thanks for putting up with them. I just feel like too Easter feels to be important. Easter is on the 21st, either the month of April or the 21st?"

"No but we were always together for Easter." "Ok. She loved to play games with you and mess with your head. I think it was a joyful thing. Tapping into her is passive aggressive sadistic but she really enjoyed it. Um. She was up for her she calls it friendly banter. She put preparation H places it should not be just because she thought it was funny like she has that kind of sense of humor."

"She put it on her face."

Laughter.

"See there you go. I know she steps forward tonight because it has been coming up a lot for you and it has been a little hard for you to move forward. It is like you get there and get there and go back a few steps. It is like you get there and get there and go back a few steps. I feel like she wanted to come forward to give you a big ole shove to say "hey it's time. You've got this, stop falling back. It's time to move forward." Oh, she is bringing you love again just so you know so she is letting you know she is bringing you love again. "She is really resistant to it." I am just listening to her right. "She is really resistant to it. She is like I don't know; I don't know. She is like no, I am winning this argument. You'll see." She wants to thank you for showing her love, for showing her kindness, and compassion. She wants to thank you for being there. She never thought in her whole life that someone would really keep their word. And you did.

Every step of the way. She said I just want to thank you for the greatest love of my life. And I will leave that with you."

Wow. Again, message received. Every detail was on point. Hearing about the lopsided mouth brought me to tears. Thinking about what she looked like after she passed always does. Despite the reminder of her suffering, hearing from her brought healing. The words chosen by Colby were eerily accurate. The word shove was deliberate. She was the one person who always knew when I needed a shove. Her timing was flawless as usual.

After the previous two readings, I was surprised she came through. My surprise gave way to gratitude for the perfectly timed shove along the healing journey. I take special joy in knowing every time she came through, her own "bunch of shit" theory was debunked and was an admission that she was wrong. Side note: Dawn's father did come through two readings later. We went two for two on date night. However, that is her story to tell.

Preparing to get remarried was exciting, but also an emotional rollercoaster. I deferred to the promises I made when the emotions were heavy. Her wish for me was nothing but happiness, even if she was not here in the physical world any longer. Three weeks prior to the last reading, my best friend from childhood, Andrea, gave the first toast at our wedding.

> *"I met Dawn nearly 40 years ago, when we were starting third grade. Throughout our angelic childhood, we forged an everlasting friendship that I know will stand the test of time. Okay Mr. Redmon, maybe angelic isn't quite the right word. Looking*

back, Dawn was fearless even as a kid (me, not so much.) So when she switched teams at the top of the fourth inning, I applauded her fearlessness. A couple years later, I was honored to witness two beautiful souls come together to become one. My heart broke in two when a short time later, one of those beautiful souls grew her angel wings. Today I have the privilege to be here with all of you to witness the start of a wonderful adventure that she so deserves with her new wife, as once again two beautiful souls become one. Dawn 2, I believe in my heart, and knew the day I met you, that you were handpicked by that angel, and I thank her for sending you! My friend has found her soulmate not once, but twice in this lifetime. As you head into the top of the 5th, I cannot imagine a more perfect love than what you two share. May your game go into extra innings!"

Perfect.

Her presence is confirmed by many who were connected to her. The pennies continue to appear in random locations, but are always perfectly timed. My last trip to the Venue was no exception. Two days before it closed its doors, Dawn and I went to one last show in the space where Yvette worked, played, and felt at home. At the end of the show, there was a penny in a wall mounted candle holder. It was not there when we arrived. Seeing the shiny, 2019, heads up coin was a testament to the beauty of endings and the reminder that with every ending a new beginning is possible.

23 - EMBRACE THE JOURNEY

Moving through life is a decision and an inevitability. Whether we embrace the task or fight it does not change the fact that our lives are always moving forward, whether we like it or not. Time passing is simple math. The number line represents our lives. We begin at zero and each moment moves us farther along the line. Counting is the easy part. Life happens in the tick marks between whole numbers. When events leave us feeling stuck, the decision to move through becomes the only viable option if peace is the goal.

Preparation only takes you so far. Bracing for disaster is one way to navigate life. Considering an alternative to white knuckling life is a starting point. What if we viewed the known and unknown as opportunities instead of roadblocks? Accepting the possibility that our precise location or circumstance exists as a way for us to grow and transform ourselves instead of holding us back is a powerful thought.

The storms in life are unavoidable. How we react to and cope with the inclement weather determines our fate. Yvette's journey of moving through began the moment she agreed to take her wellness seriously. A lifetime of shrinking took its toll. As part of her therapy, she was encouraged to journal.

Parking her feelings on those pages began her process of healing. She endured physical and emotional abuse, an eating disorder, being abandoned by her birth father, estrangement from her only child, and operating in a crippling mindset of not good enough. Her struggle was on every page. However, like a phoenix, she rose. On those pages she began to find her voice and power.

The last few entries were proof that it is never too late to address pain or trauma. Knowing Yvette was finally claiming her value made her death that much more difficult to understand. Life is hard. Life is short. Life is beautiful. While we may face difficulties, they do not have to consume us. Easier said than done, right? While hard to read, it was a testament to her courage, strength, and perseverance. The phoenix rose when she chose the process of letting go of the baggage she accumulated and carried throughout her life. She just ran out of time.

Authenticity is a word which is tossed around quite a bit. The blocks to authenticity can be removed through a variety of means. Healing past wounds is work. Hard work. We all have things which need our attention for them to heal. Learning to handle your shit is an art form. The handle your shit class syllabus includes minding your own business, filtering messages from the past, dealing with mental issues, embracing self-care, building confidence, practicing mindfulness, learning boundaries, and practicing gratitude.

If you find yourself at a crossroads and feel like finding peace and joy is not in the cards for you, just breathe. Breathing through is the precursor to moving through. After Yvette died, breathing was hard, but never ceased. Obviously. If air is flowing, you can begin changing your mindset. The decision to enact change begins with awareness. Leaning into the discomfort will shake up the dirt. The process of sifting through the pile does not need to happen overnight. Time and a constant commitment to till the land until it is ready to plant a new crop are the only tools needed. The new crop can yield abundance in every area of life if you let it.

The journey is a solo climb up the mountain and cannot be conquered in one outing. The gear you choose will sustain your ascent. Do not be afraid to ask for help along the way. Seriously, be fearless with this one. Uncovering and peeling back the accumulated layers of fear, doubt, self-loathing, perfectionism, trauma, regret, and baggage is scary. Handling your shit is inherently messy. Those with dogs or children can verify. Choosing the fight instead of flight response facilitates change.

For years, Yvette allowed her past to drain her energy. She allowed others to make all the decisions because she did not believe she was important. She felt like she had to go out of her way for everyone else in order to make her life matter. Her work ethic was driven by a need for approval. She never felt good enough, thin enough, smart enough, or like she was a successful photographer.

She accepted the unacceptable and had no idea she deserved anything other than stress, sadness, and fear. Battling fear was her main form of exercise. Seriously, she hated being sweaty and gross. The programming of the past took a toll on her mind and body but did not kill her spirit. Some days, no amount of cheerleading could convince her of her value, yet she was the biggest cheerleader to everyone else in her life. Despite her background, she was an optimist. Her story was also one of perseverance, strength, determination, and love.

Taking the lessons of the past can be painful and challenging, but worth every moment of suffering. Our moments on earth are finite, however the ability to move through infinitely betters our lives. As is true of all growing experiences, learning to move through requires practice and patience. Moving through barriers becomes second nature when you are mindful of the nature of change. Moving through is an action and a way of being. We have choices. Move through or stay stuck.

Moving through for me included allowing for the possibility of new love to come into my life before most were ready for me to do so. The truth about moving through is that no one can tell you how to do it properly. Each path is unique. Embrace the idea that you know best what moving through looks like for yourself. What is a big deal to some, may be minor to someone else. Others are irrelevant. You do you. Simple.

When the judgements or criticism begin, let them roll off your back. Standing in your truth and knowledge of what works for you is the secret to finding peace. Remember, what happens to us is not who we are. Who we are is determined by our response. Read that again. If the mind is well, we react well. Healthy environments must be created and cared for in order to have any hope of moving beyond the past.

Regardless of the belief system you may have, the universal truth remains, we are all important and have a unique place in this world. Never let someone else dictate your path. Will this make some very unhappy or angry? Yes. Remember the boundaries you set and stand firm. Even with family members. No, especially with family. Begin creating a legacy which is healthy and is based on love and kindness instead of obligation and expectation.

My journey is still unfolding. My path forward includes a new relationship, a new home, and many days of learning how to exist in my new normal. For me, Yvette's death has brought a distinct before and after in life. The before still haunts me without warning. Fortunately, my spontaneous melt downs do not phase My Dawn. I am in the best of hands when I become overwhelmed emotionally with anniversaries and the grief process.

Her father was a police officer killed in the line of duty when she was twelve. She understands how grief works. Gary D. Pagano was responding to a robbery call. The suspects tied up a maid and a child in a home. The pursuit ended when his squad car struck a vehicle parked where it should not have been. He died instantly. They were arrested and prosecuted for the robbery. That morning he left his wife and two small children to go to work and never came home. Believe me, she gets it. When I ask her when it is going to get easier, I keep hoping for an answer other than never.

Honoring Yvette's memory has meant practicing what I preach and facing my own trauma, negativity, chaos, and grief head on. But moving through also means being still sometimes. The quiet reflective stillness is how the mind readies itself to keep moving through.

My youngest began dating a girl three weeks before Yvette died. They broke up after a year and a half together. He was devastated. His loss reminded me of my own loss. Helping him navigate his grief was difficult. As he moved through his own journey, I could only hope that my example offered him comfort and hope that things get better. Encouraging him to feel his emotions and fight the urge to stuff them reinforced the moving through message so many resist.

You simply need to put one foot in front of the other, walk up, and sit at the table of your life. Look across and begin to clear off one place setting at a time. Sorry, the maid is on vacation and you will have to clean it off on your own. Some may be looking at a round table with four seats. Others may be staring down a long banquet table in a medieval castle. The size of the table may seem daunting, but you can do it. As you clean, put on some music and dance every so often.

While life tends to do what it wants, we can respond with courage and fortitude. The ability to move through pain, disappointment, loss, trauma, or just a crappy day is within us all. To truly move through, you do not need to present your life story to a theater filled with people or write a book. All you need is determination and the willingness to go deeper.

Moving Through

Remember, you are worthy of great things and your past does not define you. Whether you realize it or not, you are moving through every day. Have faith in the process and choose to take care of yourself. You will not be disappointed. The search for peace begins now.

24 - PARTING WORDS

"The original intent behind this project was to show the beauty, courage, and strength of the women I photograph. While every woman has their own story, I discovered a connection with each of them that forced me to rethink the direction I was taking.

Looking on the outside became a way for me to look deeper within me and I saw my own story playing out. I believe most people can identify with something. We all have a sameness in our struggle, victory, and the challenges we face when doubt, loss, or suffering affects our lives.

My collection of performing arts photographs show movement and detail. What my camera caught were moments of brilliance, grace, and power. My camera captured moments of true beauty, talent, and heart. However, there is always more to something than meets the eye. Even my eye missed it. Until now.

It is the story and motivation behind the work that is what matters. To the naked eye it is perfection. To truly understand the power of art for those who create it you must look beneath the surface. There you find the answers to why they dance, how they transform their own stories into movement, and the healing that happens at the end of it all.

I do the same with my photography. I was amazed to learn that my way of moving through has been reflected in the images I chose to take, and the details found in every picture. Moving through has brought me out of hiding and out of my comfort zone. The safety of staying behind the lens has felt comfortably suffocating.

My search for peace has been through photography. It has been far easier to look outward than inward. Every picture I have created has its own story. Just like all of us. My journey has brought in to focus my own strength, courage, and in the end, acceptance of myself. "

Yvette Marie Waters 6/20/69-11/26/17

Journal Wisdom

1-Hold your tongue unless it speaks to your true self.

2-The only way to make wise decisions is when you can listen to your instinct.

3-No one can ever change who you really are.

4-Change your behavior which goes against your nature.

5-Always operate out of love.

6-Forgive yourself.

7-Stop asking the fucking questions. Stop shrinking. Stop looking for someone else to tell you you're ok. You do it.

8-Love yourself more than the fear

9-Stay true to yourself. Don't let anyone or anything or any fear knock you off course.

10-Stay strong. Stay resolved. This is your life. You matter.

11-Do not go against your nature when you are afraid. Do not go against yourself.

12-It only matters what you know about yourself and who you are and how you're supposed to move through the world. Only you. No one else.

13-Your value and true nature have nothing to do with how you look.

14-Forgive yourself for the walls you build, the face you've hidden behind and the lies you've told to cover your true self up.

References

1-Manuel-Andriote, J. (2019, April). Are You the Hero or Victim of Your Story. Retrieved from https://www.psychologytoday.com/us/blog/stonewall-strong/201904/are-you-the-hero-or-victim-your-story

2- Maraboli, S. (2013). Unapologetically You: Reflections on Life and the Human Experience. Port Washington, NY: A Better Today Publishing

www.ingramcontent.com/pod-product-compliance
Lightning Source LLC
Chambersburg PA
CBHW020402080526
44584CB00014B/1130